WATERFALL WALKS
AND DRIVES
in
GEORGIA, ALABAMA
and
TENNESSEE

Published by
H.F. Publishing, Inc.
4552 E. Elmhurst Dr.
Suite A
Douglasville, Ga. 30135
U.S.A.

ISBN 0-9636070-4-9

Dedicated to my old and new-found friends in the North Fulton High School, Class of '70 and the First Friday Fraternity.

Many thanks to: Ms. Carrie Casey for identifying unidentifyable plants; Mr. William Hillary for his generousity to the public; Mr. Craig Earnest and Bowater Paper for granting public access to Virgin Falls; Mr. Talmadge Butler who beams with pride over Desoto State Park, Ala; Mr. Wayne Morrison and the staff of the South Cumberland Recreation Area; U. S. Forest Service Rangers: Mr. Johnnie Cullars, and Mr. Robert E. Lee for pointing me in the right direction; the staff of Tallulah Gorge State Park: Mr. Bill Tanner, Mr. David Perry, Ms. Brenda Cannon, Ms. Linda Lovell, Ms. Karla Rae, Ms. Christy Harvan, and Ms. Beryl Welsch; Mr. James Bowen for coaching me through projects past; Ms. Mary Robbins and Ms. Christine Cornette and the many rangers and strangers for their help with this book. Last, but not least, thanks to my wife Dee for all of her love, understanding, and support.

Front cover: a secret waterfall. Hint, it's in the book and it's in Tennessee, Nikon FM2, Nikkor 24-50 Zoom, $f/11$, Kodak Royal Gold 25, exposed @ 1 sec. Rear: Laurel Falls, Ala., Nikon FM2, Nikkor 24-50 Zoom, @ 24mm, $f/22$, Fuji Velvia, exposed @ 1 sec. B+W fill photos: pg. 24, Waterfall #2, Cloudland Canyon St. Pk., Ga.; pg. 33, Suter Falls, Savage Gulf SNA, Tn.; pg. 105, Cane Creek Falls, Fall Creek Falls St. Pk., Tn.; pg. 132, Piney Falls SNA, Tn.

Many of the more popular U. S. Forest Service Scenic Areas have become Fee Areas. They now have a nominal daily use charge.

Printed in U. S. A.

INTRODUCTION

When people from this region think of waterfalls, Amicalola Falls, Georgia, or Fall Creek Falls, Tennessee, might come to mind. These locations are very popular because of their great beauty and easy access. The intent of this book is to lead the reader to the lesser-known waterfalls in addition to these popular locations. I appreciate the "lesser knowns" for the solitude they provide. Many of them have beauty that rivals or even exceeds that of the popular spots. Most are easily reached, requiring only a little more driving or footwork. By using a little common sense, they can be safely seen.

I enjoy researching the lesser knowns, then ferreting them out. Taking a topo map and finding my way through strange woods is a real challenge to the skills I acquired as a land surveyor. Surveying is a profession that I've been out of for many years, but still have in my blood. I love landscape photography and hiking as well, so everything just fell in place, with the end result being these books.

Waterfalls are the "Gemstones of the East." Each one is faceted differently. Some have beauty that is big and bold, others have delicate and subtle characteristics. Common natural occurrences: rock, wood, and water attain their highest form when they come together as a waterfall. People who can't agree on anything else, seem to always agree on the beauty of a waterfall.

Although I know that I'm not the first to see them, there are some locations that are so pristine that I feel like I am. I have visited at least 300 waterfalls. In doing so, I've obtained directions from handouts, locals, and rangers. All too often the handouts ended up just getting me lost. I have experienced the frustration of being several miles down a road, only to find that I could go no further because of unknown road conditions, etc., while still facing miles of driving to a trailhead. I also dislike being deep into a hike only to find I can go no further, account of high water or some other unknown obstacle. If I had only known the possible conditions beforehand, I might have altered my plans (waiting a few days for waters to recede after a rain for instance). I wrote these books to provide accurate information so that you can make the most of your time.

You won't need a 4-wheel-drive vehicle or special hiking gear to visit the lesser knowns. I either drove my old Honda automobile or a small pickup. As far as hiking gear goes, you *will* need at least a pair of light hiking boots (see pg. VII for hiking essentials).

Hiking is good therapy for the pressures of modern life. The biggest challenge you'll probably face along the trail is how to cross a creek without getting your feet wet. I know this isn't as adventuresome as going to the Antarctic but if you take a closer look around you'll find new interests in things you never imagined. The woods are full of curiosities such as birds, flowers, lichens, mushrooms, and unusual rock formations. I once considered these subjects common and passé—

I now find them amazing. The more you hike, the more you'll become engrossed in things natural, both large and small.

I'm going to ask up front that you please haul out the trash that you haul in, plus whatever you find along the way. Harming natural features in any way is akin to defacing the Lincoln Memorial or other national treasures—an offense worthy of zero tolerance and strict penalties.

I'm amazed at the places that I find beer cans. I once found a can standing upright in the deep recess of a rock shelf. Someone had to get on their stomach, on wet rock, and extend their arm just as far as they could to place the can there. This is how some guys prove their manhood, I guess? I'll bet he really impressed his girl with that feat.

When To Go

Go when they flow! Many of the spectacular falls of the Cumberland Plateau (central Tennessee, northeast Alabama, and northwest Georgia) will be disappointing in the dry months of summer and fall. I therefore recommend winter and spring visits to these locations. The "T.A.G." region, as it is known, is home to the most scenic spots in the book.

I find our mild Southern winters to be the best time of year to take a hike. Yes, the days are short, and yes, there are no flowers blooming, and yes, the trees are devoid of greenery. But winter is the season of heavy rains; bright white water, blue haze-free sunny skies, no snakes, no bugs, no sweat, and no crowds. Lodging is cheap and plentiful then, too!

Trail "Mishappenings"

Don't become a victim of walking dropsy syndrome. This is where you become so enamored while looking through the camera's viewfinder, that while jockeying for a better angle, you walk off a cliff.

Watch for poisonous snakes or as my surveying buddy "Oink" Pozzi dubbed them "no shoulders," for their lack of arms and legs. It seems that once you've seen a snake every root and downed tree limb looks like another one.

Although serious and not funny at all at the time they occurred, here are some of the events I can now look back on and laugh about.

Returning from the Falls on Crow Mountain Creek, while crossing a windfallen tree trunk, I half checked a protruding root for its sturdiness as a handhold. As I crossed and placed my full weight on the root, it gave way—I ended up spread eagle in the hole of the tree's rootball. Face first in the moist clay, with my arms and legs almost pinned behind me, I flailed away doing a cross between the breast stroke and what an upside down turtle does when trying to right itself; praying all the while that some monster snake didn't share the muddy pit with me.

While en route to the Falls on Emery Creek, I chose the best route across Holly Creek. On the other side of the creek and proud of myself for staying dry, I stopped to ponder my next move. Looking down at my feet I saw a copperhead no more than two feet in front of me in the undergrowth. With downed pine tops hemming me in both left and right, I quickly walked on water back across the creek and chose a different route.

While tooling along the Panther Creek Trail, in the Cohutta Wilderness, I encountered my first wild sow. She had at least ten piglets. With one grunt, like cartoon characters with wheels spinning in midair we scratched off in opposite directions.

Yellow jackets are fun, too! While hiking in Tennessee, I took my pack off and laid it on some old in-the-trail crossties to go investigate a possible waterfall. When I returned, my pack was covered in yellow jackets. At first I thought they were after something sweet or attracted to my shiny packframe—then it dawned on me…"YELLOW JACKETS NEST IN THE GROUND!!!" With surgeon-like skill I slowly removed the pack and came away with nary a sting.

I've seen no less than five hornets' nests dangling precipitously above waterfall plunge pools. I don't know what attracts them, the water?, the open glide path?, seeking safety? From what?

I wish you good fortune and hours of hiking enjoyment. May your feet stay forever dry.

The Happy Hiker

Mark

LIKE ANY OUTDOOR ACTIVITY, "WATERFALL WALKING" ISN'T WITHOUT ITS HAZARDS. THERE HAVE BEEN SEVERAL DEATHS AND INJURIES OF THOSE TRYING TO GET A CLOSER LOOK. NEVER JEOPARDIZE YOUR SAFETY BY GETTING INTO SOMETHING YOU CAN'T GET OUT OF. SAFETY MUST BE FIRST AND FOREMOST.

Rock climbing, spelunking, white-water rafting and the like, have their own rules to minimize the risk of injury. "Waterfall Walking" has its common sense rules too.

PLEASE REMEMBER THESE DON'TS:

1. DON'T VENTURE NEAR THE CLIFF EDGE FROM WHICH THEY FALL. THERE IS NO SCENERY OVER THE EDGE, SO WHY TAKE A CHANCE?

2. DON'T GET IN THE WATER UPSTREAM FROM THE FALLS. WATER ONLY SIX INCHES DEEP, IF MOVING FAST ENOUGH, CAN KNOCK YOU OFF YOUR FEET AND TAKE YOU OVER THE EDGE. DEEP WATERS MAY *LOOK* STILL...ACTUALLY, WITH NOTHING TO IMPEDE ITS FLOW, DEEP WATER RUNS FAST.

WHEN FORDING A CREEK IN YOUR CAR, REMEMBER THAT TWO FEET OF WATER CAN SET IT AFLOAT.

3. DON'T BE FOOLED BY THE APPEARANCE OF SOLID GROUND. MOST OF THESE WATERFALL AREAS STAY PERPETUALLY WET FROM MIST AND HAVE A THIN LAYER OF LEAVES OR TOPSOIL HIDING *ALWAYS* SLICK ROCK AND POSSIBLY ICE.

4. DON'T CLIMB THEM.

5. DON'T LEAVE VALUABLES IN YOUR CAR.

6. DON'T BLOCK GATES.

But please remember to:

1. Take your camera along.

2. Bring along books on wildflowers, birds, and trees because I assure you that you'll be scratching your head, pondering the strange and beautiful sights, seen as you trek through the woods en route to these waterfalls.

3. Haul out the litter that the inconsiderate have hauled in, leaving these sites naturally unaltered.

DISCLAIMER

The author and the publisher disclaim any liability or loss incurred as a consequence, directly or indirectly, of the use and application of any information contained in this book.

*   *   *   *   *

All trail distances in this book have been measured with a Rolatape measuring wheel, except the Cable Trail at Fall Creek Falls State Park, Tn.

All of the waterfalls contained in this book except Piney and Virgin Falls, Tn. and Estatoah Falls, Ga., are located on, and accessible via public lands. Private land must be crossed to reach Piney Falls State Natural Area. Virgin Falls is a pocket wilderness owned by Bowater Paper, Inc. I have obtained permission to publish their locations and the landowners have been gracious enough to let us pass. Estatoah Falls is seen from the roadway and no trespassing is allowed. Please respect the property of others, so that we may be invited back.

HIKING ESSENTIALS

- Drinking water
- Waterproof matches
- Good light hiking boots, flip-flops to wear wading streams.
- A watch
- Flashlight
- High-energy foods
- Pocket knife
- Compass
- Benedryl or similar medicines for reactions to stings.
- Moleskin for blisters.
- While hiking, allow 30 minutes for every level mile and 1 hour for every 1000' gain in elevation.

Snake bites

Pit Vipers: Venom causes necrosis and pain. Treat with light constricting band and Sawyer Extractor. No cut and suck. Treat the wound, calm the victim, immobilize the extemity and evacuate for antivenin.

Coral Snake: Same treatment as above.

CONTENTS

Desoto State Park - Little River Canyon National Preserve, Alabama

Cumberland Plateau, Tennessee

Cherokee National Forest (Southern Districts), Tennessee

Addendum

HOW TO USE THIS BOOK

This text is keyed to its maps and begins its coverage in northwestern Georgia. Progressing eastward, the book gives full coverage to north Georgia's Chattahoochee National Forest. The text then picks up in northeastern Alabama and ventures into the Cumberland Plateau of central Tennessee. The final chapter covers the southern districts of the Cherokee National Forest in east Tennessee.

This book will lead you from a prominent landmark or intersection to individual waterfalls. Where several waterfalls are in close proximity to one another, they are listed in the order in which they are encountered from that landmark or intersection (see Helen - Hiawassee Area pgs. 48-49).

Note in this example that #1, Ga. Hwy. 356 East, is 1.1 miles from the Chattahoochee River Bridge in downtown Helen, and that #3 (F.S. 44) is 9.4 miles. To find the distance between them, simply subtract. The two points are 8.3 miles apart. In the same example if you wanted to drive from #9 (the intersection of U.S. 76), to #5 (F.S. 283), your distance would be 18.4 minus 11.5 equaling 6.9 miles.

Listed along with each waterfall is:

(1) The worst road conditions encountered: Graveled, etc. (See the example below.)

(2) A beauty scale of 1 (worth seeing), through 10 (a knockout).

(3) The waterfall's height (if known).

(4) The U.S.G.S. topographic map or other such map that was used in reference.

(5) The official trail number (if known).

(6) The one-way hiking distance and/or time required to reach them (also noted in the text). Round-trip distances will be noted as such.

(7) Water crossings (if any) and the effort needed to reach the falls (very easy, through difficult). See definitions.

---

(1) Roads: Graveled   (2) A "10"   (3) 30'
(4) U.S.G.S. Quadrangle: Tray Mtn., Ga.
(5) Trail #, (6) .8 of a mile, (7) water crossing, moderate

DEFINITIONS:

Carsonite stake: A trade name for a fiberglass-type stake used to mark roads and trails.

Path: An unmaintained treadway.

Trail: A maintained treadway.

Very Easy: A smooth path over level ground.

Easy: Uneven ground, but fairly level.

Moderate: Some steep grades, some level sections of trail.

Difficult: Steep grades, uneven terrain and long, steady climbs.

Graveled: A road that most automobiles without airdams could negotiate, except where noted.

High Clearance: A road that most pickup trucks could negotiate.

U.S.G.S. Quadrangle: A U.S. Geological Survey topo map.

ABBREVIATIONS:

BT = The Bartram Trail
CRT = The Chattooga River Trail
SDL = The Savage Day Loop
SNA = State Natural Area
SR = The South Rim Trail
F.S. = Forest Service, designating a Forest Service road.

KEY TO MAP SYMBOLS:

★ = A landmark from which the text begins.

A,1,b, etc.: Italicized letters or numbers on Area Maps represent waterfall locations or landmarks with mileage given in the text. Numbers subdivide capital letters; lower case letters subdivide numbers, etc.

Contour intervals on hiking maps are 200′ unless otherwise noted.

▬▬▬▬▬▬	Paved Roads
▬ ▬ ▬ ▬ ▬ ▬	Graveled or Dirt Roads
▬ ▬ ▬ ▬ ▬ ▬	Trails
▬▬ • • • ▬▬	Rivers and Creeks
P	Parking
●—●	Gate

PHOTOGRAPHING WATERFALLS

Most people don't seem to associate photography with work. My guess is that they associate "taking pictures" with being on vacation (having fun). "How could that be work?" they must ask themselves. I think you'll find serious photography very hard work. The knowledge of how to use cameras, lenses, and films takes a great deal of time and expense to acquire. Lugging equipment into remote locales and up and down mountainsides is sometimes arduous. Standing in the midst of breathtaking scenery and capturing it on film with the results *you* want is ample reward for the hardships often endured.

Good images take careful planning. In the case of waterfalls, being there at the right time is of the utmost importance. During dry periods, usually summer and fall, or under drought conditions, many locations have greatly reduced water flows that make them less photogenic. Also with this high-contrast subject, you must utilize the best natural lighting conditions.

Successful photography begins with a good camera system. There are several brands and camera models in the 35mm format that fit the bill. I prefer a manual camera such as the Nikon FM2 for its simplicity and wide array of available accessories.

Many of these waterfalls have to be photographed closely because of view-blocking rocks, trees, and vegetation. The 46° field of view of a normal lens (50mm) in most cases is not wide enough. Nikon makes a 24-50mm wide-angle zoom lens which is ideal for most waterfall photography, having an 84 to 46° range of coverage. This lens also has macro capabilities making it useful in photographing wildflowers as well. (Watch carefully for lens flare with this lens. This condition may not be readily apparent through the viewfinder, but during long exposures it will be on film.)

Use a tripod and shutter-release cable at all shutter speeds. This eliminates the possibility of camera shake and ensures the sharpest images. These items also allow you to make long exposures for smooth-flowing, velvet-like water.

Depth of field: Generally, depth of field falls 1/3 in front of, and 2/3 behind the object of focus. For example if the object of focus is 50′ away, the nearest object in sharp focus would be 33′, while the farthest object would be 83′. All objects within that range will be in sharp focus. Focusing in this way wastes alot of depth of field.

To remedy this, stop the lens down. Apertures of *f*/8 to *f*/22 yield greater depth of field and thus sharper images. Learn how to set the depth of field for any given aperture. It's very simple to do and you can obtain images that are sharp from front to back by setting your lens properly. For example, on my 50mm lens set at *f*/22, if I set the far depth-of-field distance (infinity on the focusing ring, in this example) in line with *f*/22 on the far depth-of-field scale, the near depth-of-field distance automatically lines up with *f*/22 on the *near* depth-of-field scale, and reads 6 1/2′. (This yields a "hyperfocal distance" [where the object of focus lies] of 12 1/2′.) This means that all objects between 6 1/2′ and infinity will be in sharp focus. Even though the scene appears out of focus in the viewfinder, it will be rendered on film with front-to-back sharpness. Compose the shot with this in mind, keeping objects that are too close (since they would be out of focus on film) out of the frame. Better cameras like the FM2 have a depth-of-field preview button to let you see the stopped-down results in advance.

Metering: Try to shoot in evenly-lighted conditions. High-contrast lighting produces poor photos. Master photographer Galen Rowell teaches that "…our eyes have an eleven-stop light range…" and that films simply can't record this wide tonal range. In order to come away with the best images we need to "…learn to see as the film sees.…"

Print films can "see" a range of light, or have a *latitude* of 7 stops, with 5 stops being optimum. Slide films have a 5 stop latitude, with 3 being optimum. Meter your subject with this in mind. If there is an area in the viewfinder that is either too bright, or too dark, recompose the shot to eliminate the unwanted area or wait for even lighting. Remember that with most cameras the viewfinder only covers around 93% of a scene or you may inadvertently include part of the unwanted area.

When metering, leave the waterfall out of the equation. Meter for the "averagely" lit rock and/or light-green foliage around the waterfall. If you meter for the much brighter waterfall itself, you'll end up with gray water and silhouettes of the surroundings. For more accurate exposures use an 18% gray card in the same light as the subject. You may have a camera bag that is close enough to 18% gray to use in lieu of a gray card.

When using slow films in very low-light conditions, you can obtain a useable shutter speed by switching the camera's film speed dial to a faster film speed setting. If for instance you are using 50 speed film, set the aperture on your lens to obtain the depth of field you desire, then set the film speed dial to, let's say, 200 (used here for ease of calculation, you can use 100, 400, 1000, or whatever film speed setting it takes to get a reading). Take a meter reading of an averagely-lit area in the scene. Now multiply that reading by 4, since 50 divided into 200 = 4. If you had a shutter speed reading of say, 1 second, expose the film for 4 seconds. If your camera's shutter speed dial doesn't allow for exposures of over 1 second, set the dial to the "bulb" setting and time the shot yourself, by counting, one thousand one, one thousand two, etc. (Afterward, be sure to reset the film speed dial back to your correct film speed setting to avoid later metering errors.)

Films are engineered to react to light within certain parameters. When used outside of these time frames, they react differently, i.e. colors may not be true, contrast changes, or the film may be underexposed. Call or write the film's manufacturer for a data sheet which gives details of the film's characteristics, including "reciprocity failure." Reciprocity failure is the failure of film to record light accurately when used outside the limits for which it was designed. With Fujichrome Velvia and Provia films there is no correction needed for exposures of 4 seconds or less. With Kodachrome 25 and 64 speed films add 1/2 and 1 stop respectively when exposing at 1 second or your shots will come out underexposed.

Exposure: To show the power of a large waterfall, stop the action with the use of a medium speed film, ISO 100 or 200, and a fast shutter speed, 1/125ᵀᴴ of a second or faster. Plan to shoot on a bright, sunny day so that the sharper, small apertures can be used. In general, large powerful waterfalls look unnatural when long exposures are used. With lots of water, long exposures may "wash out" the film, leaving the waterfall featureless.

Smaller waterfalls photograph better under shady or overcast conditions. This allows the use of small apertures for sharpness and long exposures to softly blur the water. Use films rated ISO 25 to 100 for their long exposure tolerances and fine grain. With smaller waterfalls there is less chance of washing the film out. It's hard to obtain good shots on windy days using slow shutter speeds unless you can exclude the movement of vegetation.

Bracket your shots. Expose at the correct meter reading, then expose at least 1 stop over and 1 stop under in 1/2 stop increments. This assures that you'll have at least one correctly exposed shot.

Composition: Fill the frame with your subject. I have often made the mistake of trying to include too much in a photo, with the end result being a dinky waterfall lost among the other detail.

On sunny days a rainbow may be found in the mist in an arc that hangs 42° from the antisolar point. The antisolar point lies exactly 180° opposite the sun and is marked by the shadow of the observer's head.

The "rule of thirds" works well in waterfall photography. This common composition technique catches, then leads the eye into a photo. Divide the viewfinder into thirds with two imaginary vertical lines and then two imaginary horizontal lines—like a tic-tac-toe board. When shooting either vertically or horizontally place the subject at or near one of the four positions where these lines cross. Compose the shot with the waterfall flowing freely into and across the frame.

Avoid "Keystoning" if possible. This occurs when the camera is tilted up or down. (In the case of most waterfalls since we will be at the base looking up, I'll use the following example.) Since the subject is closer to the film plane at the bottom and farther away at the top, it appears much larger at the bottom and smaller at the top (like a pyramid, or inverted keystone) than our naked eyes see it. Wide-angle lenses exaggerate this distortion. To avert this, try shooting the subject straight on (parallel to the film plane) if possible. Special lenses called perspective-control, or "PC" lenses correct this distortion to a degree, but they are expensive.

Films: I almost always shoot slide film for the sharpness and intense colors it is capable of recording. I'm partial to Fujichrome Velvia (50 speed) and Provia (100 speed) films for their fine grain, true colors, and ease of processing. These films have good latitude and are able to handle highlight and shadow detail better than other films.

Many times the 50 or 100 speed rating of these films is not fast enough for the conditions I'm shooting in. If I need the extra speed, to freeze action or for increased depth of field, I push these films by 1 stop. This is done by changing the camera's film speed setting. With 50 speed film, set the meter to 100 and with 100 speed film set it to 200. The film is thus underexposed by 1 stop in the camera. To compensate for this, it must be overexposed or "pushed" by 1 stop in the first developer during processing. Mark the cassette as such and be sure to ask for push processing, which is slightly more expensive. I would rather push Velvia or Provia films by 1 stop than use their faster rated contemporaries for two reasons: 1. they cost less; 2. the faster films just can't match Velvia's or Provia's fine grain and image quality.

If you need to slow a film down, use a polarizing filter. A polarizing filter will reduce the light entering the lens by 1 to 2 stops allowing for longer exposure times. Carefully turn the filter and observe its effect on the wet rock, foliage, and the blue sky (which will be rendered a deeper blue if the camera is pointed at right angles to the sun). This filter, through its glare reduction, saturates the film with color and thus enhances the image. If this filter is used improperly the rock's glistening sheen will look flat and unnatural. A neutral density filter will reduce light also, but I find a polarizer far more handy.

In early morning and late afternoon lighting, slide films will record the surroundings with a steely-blue cast. This occurs because daylight-balanced films are designed to be used in the interim between 2 hours after sunrise and 2 hours before sunset when warmer light is present. This blue cast can be corrected with a warming filter.

Kodak Royal Gold 25 and 100 speed color negative films are the best I've found for prints. These films have fine grain, great sharpness, and excellent colors.

For black-and-white photography I like Kodak T-Max 100 speed negative film for its sharpness. This film can also be pushed 1 stop without having to overdevelop to compensate for its underexposure. This means that the film speed can be switched from 100 to 200 in mid-roll if you need the additional speed for increased depth of field or to freeze action. This switch is not possible with slide or color negative films.

Black and white or color print films can bail you out in bad lighting situations. These films can record the shots that slide films can't. Negative film can be overexposed in the field then manipulated in the printing process to obtain the detail you actually saw in the field.

Misc. conditions: In the cold of winter you may run into the unattractive curling of rhododendron leaves. This self corrects as daytime temperatures rise.

Camera care: After use, be sure that you have not left the shutter cocked as this could stretch the return springs. Set the lens' aperture to its widest opening to ensure that the blades don't become bent. Keep your camera clean and dry.

Affordable Photography

We all know how expensive photographic equipment is. Over the years I've found ways to cut costs down to less painful levels. Here are some of them.

Most people who know me, know that I'm a tightwad. I admit it. Yes, I am a tightwad, but I'm no cheapskate! When I buy most anything, I look for the best product at the lowest possible price. So when shopping for camera equipment, films, and the like, I shop mail order. In most cases you'll save at least 30%. (And being interstate commerce, most states levy no sales tax.) You will incur shipping and insurance fees, so you'll want to place an order large enough to justify those expenses. Here's what to do.... Purchase the latest edition of your favorite photography magazine. Many of them have the whole back section devoted to mail order ads. Look for a magazine that has ads for B+H Photo or Adorama, Inc. Both are New York based and carry most everything. I've had good results with them both. If for some reason I did have a problem, and they were at fault, they've promptly refunded both the purchase price of the item and shipping fees. When ordering, ask whether all items are in stock. If an item is not in stock you may have to wait for a back order. It's a good idea to order well ahead of your expected time of need. Generally though, most in-stock items (which most are) will be at your door within a week's time. As I said, you'll save money with mail order, but it still pays to comparison shop. On occasion I have found some items for less at local camera shops.

To save money on film...roll your own! You can purchase 100' rolls of cold-stored professional films by mail order at far less cost than off-the-shelf films. One-hundred feet will yield 18, 36 frame rolls with leaders. You'll need an Alden 74 or similar 35mm bulk film loader. You'll also need film cassettes. For the long term, buy the best reloadable cassettes you can find. Pass up the cheap ones as they may leak light or scratch your film. Not counting the initial cost of the bulk loader and cassettes, you'll save up to 50% over factory-loaded films.

When ordering, insist on fresh film with an expiration date far into the future.

When you can...cut the middleman

Film processing is another area where you can save big bucks. I never take my hard earned photos to a drug store. I gave up on them long ago after having some of my best shots ruined. Instead, I send my factory-loaded cassettes (slides or prints) to Kodak or Fuji for their in-house processing. I purchase Kodalux or Fuji "mailers" by mail order. Mailers are pre-paid in-house processing envelopes from those respective companies. Kodalux is the licensee for processing Kodachrome films. Photo labs, since they lack the license, serve only as middlemen who collect and forward this film to Kodalux. Usually they charge a hefty "handling fee" when they have done nothing more than put your film in the mail for you. After postage is added in, mailers will save you 40% over most retail lab services. The trade-off is that it takes 2-3 days longer to receive the slides back since we're low volume customers.

A hot mailbox can ruin your film. Be safe, use the indoor box at the post office.

I take the cassettes that I load myself to a reputable local lab for processing and ask that they return my cassettes.

If you want to try your hand at printing negatives look in the yellow pages under "Photographic Darkroom Rental" to see if your city has rental darkrooms. Prints are expensive, but again you can save big bucks over having a lab do them for you. You'll also learn creative printing techniques such as dodging and burning. The people that staff these darkrooms are very knowledgeable and helpful.

Some darkrooms have "Tray Rooms" where for a fee you can bring your favorite paper and chemistry for superior results. In most cases though, you'll have to buy paper from them.

Suggested reading: *"Galen Rowell's Vision,"* and *"John Shaw's Landscape Photography."*

LaFayette Area

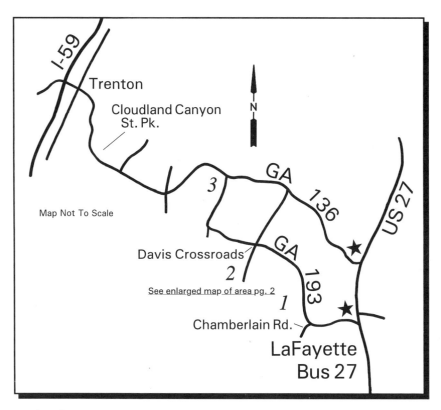

Directions: From the intersection of Bus. 27 and Ga. Hwy. 193 North in downtown LaFayette, take Hwy. 193 North to the following points of interest:

1. Chamberlain Road, access to Rocktown Scenic Area: 2.8 miles.
2. Hog Jowl Road (Davis Crossroads), access to the Falls on Pocket Branch: 8.2 miles.
3. Ga. Hwy. 136 (alternate directions to Cloudland Canyon State Park): 13.6 miles. From this intersection drive west on Hwy. 136 for 8.0 miles to the entrance to Cloudland Canyon State Park.

1. Rocktown Scenic Area, Pigeon Mountain, Walker County, Georgia

Roads: Graveled   No falls at this location.
U.S.G.S. Quadrangle: Cedar Grove, Ga.
Pink blazed, 1.1 miles, easy

Directions: Turn left (south) onto Chamberlain Road and drive 3.5 miles to Rocky Lane (sign: "Crockford - Pigeon Mountain Wildlife Management Area").

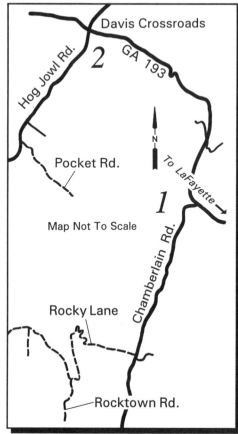

Turn right and travel up the steep mountainside for 4.95 miles to Rocktown Road which is on the left. There may be a carsonite stake here reading "Rocktown Road—Dead End." (There is another road in the vicinity of 4.75 miles which is also on the left—please don't confuse it with the correct route.) Drive Rocktown Road for .65 of a mile to its end. The trail begins at the information board on the west side of the parking area.

Before entering the woods bone up on the area's geological history at the information board.

Enter the woods and in 120' cross a small branch on a footbridge. The pink-blazed trail starts up and bends left to round the hillside. In .1 of a mile the trail levels off as it joins a roadbed. Passing through a forest dominated by small hardwoods, the treadway is heavily lined in galax and haircap moss. For the next .1 of a mile the trail again ascends at an easy rate to a high point where it then levels off. At .35 of a mile arrive at a large boulder on the right. This is just a small sampling of what's ahead.

Many of these sandstone boulders have been eroded by wind and water to resemble giant pulled teeth standing on their roots—huge molars, complete with cavities, that teeter on a too-small base.

Near the half-mile point the trail turns sharply left at a boulder outcrop seen approximately 150' to the right of the trail. From here on, albeit sporadically, the boulders increase in number. Nearing the 1 mile point, after a brief absence, the boulders reappear in larger form on both the left and right sides of the trail. At 1.1 miles the official trail ends and exploratory pathways disperse among the two-story rock giants.

Having been pockmarked by wind and stained with the varnish of leaching minerals, many of these gigantean sandstone boulders resemble large meteorites.

Where moisture and shade allow, brilliant-green mosses and gray lichens have colonized and lent their colors to the weathered, brick-red rock. Trees and

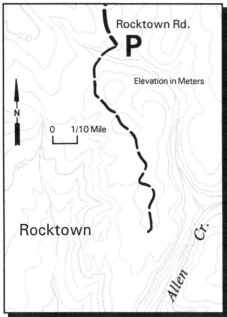

shrubbery have taken root in cracks where soil has collected. In places, beautifully deformed trees have grown up ten feet or more before becoming fused with the overhead rock. Other boulders overhang, with cleft rock poised ready to fall. Several boulders form maze-like, dead-end passages while others have splits too narrow for passage.

Some of the trees native to the area are: black tupelo, hickory, big-leaf magnolia, pine, and several varieties of oak. To get an open view and better grasp of Rocktown's enormity, I suggest you visit when the leaves are off.

2. Falls on Pocket Branch, Walker County, Georgia

Roads: Graveled   A "4" 20'
U.S.G.S. Quadrangle: Cedar Grove, Ga.
.4 of a mile, easy-moderate

Note: Best seen after prolonged periods of rainfall. I'm sure this wet-weather waterfall would be very beautiful when complimented by the greens of spring and summer—provided there was adequate rainfall.

Directions: Turn left onto Hog Jowl Road and drive 2.75 miles (passing Mt. Hermon Baptist Church) to Pocket Road. Turn left onto Pocket Road (sign: "Dead End"), after traveling .4 of a mile the pavement ends. Pass the Crockford - Pigeon Mountain Wildlife Management Area sign at .95 of a mile. Ford a small unnamed branch at 1.2 miles then look for the parking area just ahead on the left. The hike begins at the information board just east of the parking area. There is a carsonite stake here stating, "Pocket Loop Trail." This trail is blue blazed. The trail to the falls is orange blazed but shares the same treadway.

Hike the gated road which leads southeast and in approximately 100' pass the gate. The trail ascends the graveled roadbed and at .15 of a mile passes beautiful

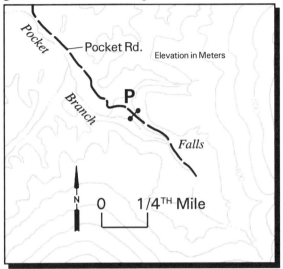

gray, fortress-like cliffs on the left. Beech, oak, poplar, and sycamore crowd the slope between the road and the foot of these cliffs. Cedar trees populate the craggy cliff tops. The cliffs diminish in size as the road continues ascending. At .33 of a mile arrive at a point where the falls are viewed frontally from the road. A slim side trail leads down then levels on its way to their base.

The falls consist of two slim broken flows over gray and off-white limestones. The left flow is the more vertical of the two. The right flow cascades through a chute. The mineral-laden waters have formed tufa, much like the terraced mineral deposits at the hot springs of Yellowstone National Park, only these are of the rare cold-water variety. Instead of being terraced, these deposits look like the rippled folds in drapery. These deposits are evident in the rock face between the two flows.

Aside from being unusual, the surrounding area is very beautiful. The limestone cliffs show hundreds of different layers. The creek has cut a V-shaped channel in the cliffs through which it falls. Steep hillsides top the 20' cliffs adjacent to the falls. Algae in and around the falls has stained the rock an olive drab color.

To reach the top area, hike the road another 280' to a flat spot beside them.

3. Ga. Hwy. 136 (as above).

Cloudland Canyon State Park, Dade County, Georgia

Roads: Paved, Ga. fee area
U.S.G.S. Quadrangle: Durham, Ga.
Waterfall Trail: blue blazed, see text for distances, difficult
West Rim Trail: yellow blazed, 4.9 miles round trip, moderate

Note: The infirm, or persons with heart or respiratory problems should not attempt the steep hike to the falls.

This is a great place to visit in winter, for the water; in spring, for the wildflowers; in summer, for the fun of it; and in fall, for the colors.

Directions: From U.S. 27 and Ga. Hwy. 136, north of LaFayette, drive west on 136 for 17.4 miles to the park's entrance. Turn right, driving 1.45 miles to the parking area for the trails listed below.

Alternate directions: See Item #3 under the Area Map at the beginning of this chapter.

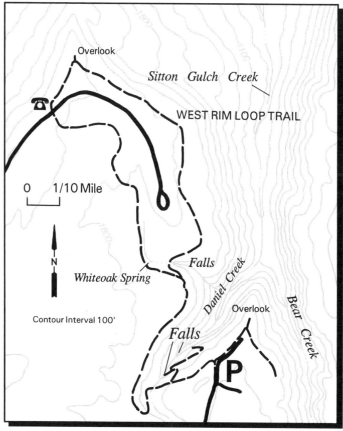

Rim Trails: These trails begin between the #2 and #3 picnic shelters, 25' left of the information board. From the parking area, steps lead 135' to the rim. There, the East Rim Trail splits right and the West Rim Loop Trail splits left. From this vantage point in the wetter months while looking northwest across the canyon, a two-tier waterfall is seen leaping from the rim. Also, the top of Waterfall #2 may be seen below.

East Rim Trail: This paved trail is the park's easiest and holds a preview of things to come. First, a view of Daniel Creek Canyon, then due north of the concession stand, a side trail leads 300' to an overlook where the cliffs of Sitton Gulch and Bear Creek Canyon are seen. After visiting the overlook return to the Rim Trail and continue southeast where Bear Creek's Canyon may be further studied.

From the rim trails the stratigraphy of these canyons is clearly visible. The softer shale layers have abundant vegetation, while the harder sandstones have none. There is an excellent self-guiding booklet on the park's geology, the *Geologic Guide to Cloudland Canyon State Park* by Martha M. Griffin and Robert L. Atkins, available at park headquarters.

Bridge/West Rim Loop Trail: At the rim this trail turns immediately left then right and at 450' (from the parking area) passes behind cabins 5 through 1. Leaving the cabins the trail soon turns sharply right and descends into the canyon. At the quarter-mile point, after descending a small flight of steps, arrive where the Bridge/West Rim Loop Trail splits left and the Waterfall Trail splits right. (See Waterfall Trail, below.)

The Bridge/West Rim Loop Trail continues its descent at a moderate rate over rock and in-ground steps, passing scenic sandstone outcrops on the left and through laurel and Catawba rhododendron. At one third of a mile arrive alongside Daniel Creek. The trail bends left and follows the creek upstream. At .4 of a mile cross the creek on a wooden footbridge for which the trail is named. From the bridge the now solo West Rim Trail bends sharply left and climbs moderately following Daniel Creek upstream. In 300', confronted with a scenic rock bluff, the trail turns sharply right, ascends a short distance, then levels off. At .55 of a mile the trail makes a sharp bend left at a weeping rock outcrop, then switchbacks up to tread the canyon's rim.

In the drier microclimate of the rim, chestnut and blackjack oak reside, along with maple and mountain laurel. Atop the rim the trail turns right. In .1 of a mile tread over a spot of bedrock then cross a small branch. Just ahead the parking area, overlooks, and stairs leading to the falls are seen across the canyon. Between .8 and .9 of a mile huge sandstone boulders litter the slopes below.

The next landmark is the white-blazed campground trail which leads left at .95 of a mile. At just over 1 mile investigate the large boulders that have sheared away from the cliff. These will one day topple into the canyon like those seen along the Waterfall Trail. Shallow depressions and wave-like ripples suggest that this rock was formed in a tidal flat. The view up Daniel Creek's Canyon from atop the boulders is very scenic.

The trail treads a sandy stretch then at 1.15 miles arrives at the first area protected by railing. Soon thereafter the trail bends left to outline the hollow of Whiteoak Spring Branch (the small creek that gives rise to the wet-weather waterfall seen at the beginning of the hike). At 1.3 miles, deep in this hollow, arrive at the loop trail which begins and ends at the footbridge over Whiteoak Spring Branch.

Hiking in a counterclockwise direction with a cumulative distance, at 1.5 miles the trail completes its outline of the hollow and winds up directly across the canyon from the parking area. The cliffs of Bear Creek Canyon are now in full view as well. A side trail at 1.6 miles leads to overlooks of Daniel and Bear Creek Canyons and the first good glimpse of Sitton Gulch.

From this double overlook the loop trail turns 90° to the left and enters a wooded area of pine and small oaks. For the next .5 of a mile (with the exception of a couple of paths leading to the rim) the trail leaves the rim for deeper woods. The now drier slopes support no laurel or rhododendron and as well, the trees are smaller. At 2.15 miles there is a spot where, while looking north, the farms in the Lookout Valley can be seen below. The trail meanders while ascending from a hollow. At 2.55 miles reach the apex of the loop. Look for a side trail leading right for 100' down to an overlook of the farms in the valley to the north and the gradually sloping plateau to the east.

The loop trail turns sharply left here and follows the crest of the ridge southwesterly. After passing through small stands of the beautiful fringetree (covered with sweet smelling, white blooms in early spring), scrub oak, and pine, at 2.65 miles pass through a jumble of large boulders. The trail winds in an S fashion through them. This is the highest point of the hike. The trail veers left at 2.75 miles. (Signs here warn the hiker not to wander off the trail.) Descending from this point, at 2.8 miles cross a footbridge then a paved road and reenter the piney woods. The trail now meanders while descending into a hollow of small hardwoods with tree sparkleberry set among them. At 2.95 miles the trail turns sharply left and crosses a lesser hollow then bends right to follow its east side. At 3.05 miles cross to the main hollow's west side and soon thereafter pass an unusually shaped boulder on the right. At 3.15 miles the trail bends left as an old roadbed intersects from the right. In one-fourth mile cross a 5'-wide creek on steppingstones and pass the walk-in tent camping access trail.

The trail now descends, albeit distantly, along the west side of the creek. After crossing a small hollow the trail nears the creek and both bend sharply left among the beech trees, holly, and laurel. At just over 3.6 miles tie back into the beginning of the loop.

Waterfall Trail: From the trail split, the Waterfall Trail descends into the canyon via a series of staircases and boardwalks. In winter these structures can be real bun busters due to icing. In 300' pass beneath a huge sandstone overhang with lesser shale layers visible under its mass. Pick up the stairs again and continue descending. At 700' reach the junction of the 1ST and 2ND Waterfall Trails. Veer left towards the 1ST Falls. Just shy of .2 of a mile, massive boulders are seen on the creek's west side as are beautiful cliffs on the left (east side) with the scenic creek below. Round a bend (the cliffs) to the left and after passing through a gradually widening root-laced and rocky stretch, at one-fourth mile, arrive at the base of the 1ST Falls.

The 1ST Falls are approximately 10' wide in full flow and resemble others found on the Cumberland Plateau. They fall a sheer 50' into a large plunge pool in a bowl-shaped cirque. The cliffs of this cirque are 60-70' high. Their base is littered with talus. Look for American holly, hemlock, oak, rhododendron, and shagbark hickory around the pool area.

2ND Falls: From the 1ST Fall's Trail junction, the 2ND Falls Trail descends via steep staircases and over boardwalks. Between 150 and 200' the trail passes under a rock wall and dripping overhang that wets part of the boardwalk. Again, watch for ice in winter. Daniel Creek, seen far below, is lined with massive boulders. The descent into the canyon between 300 and 800' is especially beautiful. After hiking .25 of a mile from the 1ST Fall's Trail junction arrive at the 2ND Fall's observation deck.

The 2ND Falls drop a sheer 90' over a lip of overhanging rock. When seen from the deck, a large sandstone boulder blocks much of the right portion from view. The cirque is approximately 200' across with a small plunge pool on the right side of this immense opening.

Villanow Area

Keown Falls Scenic Area, Walker County, Georgia

Roads: Graveled   Scenic Area A "10"
U.S.G.S. Quadrangle: Sugar Valley, Ga.
Keown Falls Loop Trail #20, 1.6 miles, water crossing, moderate
Johns Mountain Loop Trail #66, 3.1 miles, water crossing, moderate

Note: Scenic area gated Nov. 15 to Apr. 15.

I went to this area after a period of heavy summer rainfall. I did so because I had read that there was little or no water much of the year. Even though there had been a great deal of recent rainfall, the two waterfalls were still only a trickle. Being high on the ridge and spring fed, long periods of steady rain are needed to recharge the water table in this region of porous limestone and sandstone. A local hiker told me that after winter rains the falls are quite impressive.

Directions: From the intersection of Ga. Hwys. 136 and 201 in the community of Villanow, drive east on 136 (passing the Forest Service work station) for .3 of a mile to Pocket Road. Turn right and drive 5.0 miles to F.S. 702 (sign:

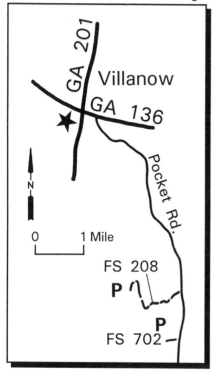

"Keown Falls Scenic Area"). Turn right and travel .65 of a mile to the parking area and trailhead.

At the trailhead there is a sign telling whether the falls are flowing or not. Make this hike be they wet or dry, for the outstanding feature here is not the waterfalls but the magnificent rock bluffs and the vistas from atop them. The falls are a bonus. The overlook atop Keown Falls is *the* place to be for fall foliage.

Enter the woods at the information board and pass under an A-frame. Here, you make the transition from the civilized world into the wild—a symbolic welcome to the woods. The trail is well constructed and the first portion, which passes through a picnic area, is graveled and lined with stone. The trail splits to form a loop at .1 of a mile. I hiked the loop in a counterclockwise direction, as it appears to be the most heavily traveled section.

The hardwood forest on the lower slopes is youthful but very scenic. Its floor is littered with hundreds of small boulders. More mature stands of dogwood, hickory, maple, chestnut and red oak, as well as poplar are higher up the mountainside.

At .3 of a mile the trail closely follows a small branch. Just ahead it crosses this branch then turns sharply left. Next, the trail starts steeply uphill via a switchback, first right, then back left. The left bend is protected with a split-rail fence. Slightly more than .4 of a mile into the hike, the trail makes a sharp right bend in an area of large boulders. Notice the rocky creek below and the cliffs on its south side. At .6 of a mile the trail turns sharply left (there may be a bench here for the weary). In another .1 of a mile the trail climbs a stone stairway then encounters boulders and cliffs of stratified sand and limestones. Mosses, lichens, and wind-twisted pines enhance these already beautiful rock exposures.

Just ahead a stairway on the right accesses the Johns Mountain Trail. (There may be a sign here "Johns Mountain Loop Trail 2.5 miles, Overlook 1 Mile.") Make a side trip of 100' up this connector trail to a cliff-top observation deck

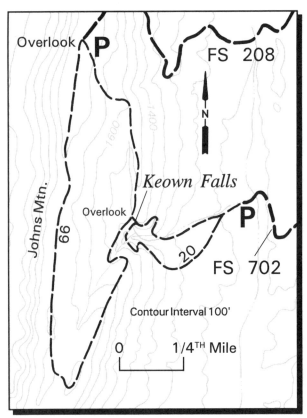

Overlook

FS 208

N

Keown Falls

Overlook

P

FS 702

Contour Interval 100'

Johns Mtn.

66

20

0   1/4ᵀᴴ Mile

and one of the most beautiful vistas in Georgia. (Also see Johns Mountain Loop Trail, below*.)

Looking southeast you have a clear view of Horn Mountain in the distance. This is a great spot to hangout on a fall afternoon and photograph while the western sun bathes the colorful mountain slopes in warm light. The viewpoint also overlooks the cove of Keown Falls, which is a masterpiece in itself.

Return to the Keown Falls Trail and continue towards the falls. At just over .7 of a mile arrive at a high point where the falls first come into view. Note the deep and colorful cave-like alcove with 30' cliffs on either end. The cliff face is more than 100' wide with talus littering its base. The falls lightly shower the rubble below. Their splattering sound resonates from the alcove's depths.

Continuing, pass behind the falls then by a 40' cliff with square, neatly-fissured rock. Eight tenths of a mile into the hike encounter a dripping rock overhang. This is sort of a mini version of the falls just visited. Just ahead is a stretch of weeping rock with ferns below. At .9 of a mile reach the highest point on the trail and what I consider the second most beautiful sight in this scenic area—a rock wall with only a spout of water flowing over it. Again, it's not the water that makes this a grand sight, but the colorful mosses and lichens adorning the cliffs and talus.

Leaving the spout-type falls, in 100' the trail turns left and begins to switchback down the rocky slope. Just shy of a mile notice an unusually shaped oak tree approximately 70' off the trail on the right. This tree grows out of the boulders and looks to have been gnarled by the wind. Descending still further via bends and a switchback, the trail becomes more conducive to hiking as it once again enters the openness of the young forest. Stones again line the trail as you near a small oak tree with a huge gall. At 1.5 miles rejoin the inbound portion of the loop. A right turn leads back to the parking area.

Johns Mountain Loop Trail

Directions: From F.S. 702 (the access road to Keown Falls) drive north on Pocket Road for .95 of a mile to F.S. 208. Turn left and drive 2.2 miles to the parking area at Johns Mountain Overlook. The white-blazed trail enters the woods on the southeast corner of the parking lot and ties back in at the southwest corner. For an easy to moderate hike, hike this trail in a clockwise direction.

Slightly descending for the first 100', the trail ties into an old roadbed, turns right and descends still further. For the next 600' the trail descends at a moderate rate while passing scenic boulder outcrops and laurel thickets. At .25 of a mile cross a small spring-like branch which rises beside the trail. The woods here consist of small- to medium-size pine trees scattered about the blueberry and sweetshrub understory. At .35 of a mile the trail bends sharply right and heads due south. Still descending, pass a scenic rock outcrop on the left and a pathway leading to its viewing area.

The loop trail descends along the left side of a hollow and at .45 of a mile levels off somewhat. At .6 of a mile the trail makes a hard right in the vicinity of a road that intersects from the left. At .75 of a mile, 120' to the trail's east are the ruins of an old homestead. There is a concrete pillar here and the remnants of what looks like a stone chimney. Twenty feet south of the chimney is a stone wall that runs east and west.

The trail continues to wind along the east side of the hollow. Among the hollow's ferns the fall's branch is born. This is the largest gathering of ferns I've yet to encounter—probably two acres in size. At .8 of a mile the Johns Mountain Loop turns right then crosses the fall's branch. *A trail to the left here leads to an observation deck 70' away, then connects with the Keown Falls Loop Trail.

Leaving the overlook area the Johns Mountain Loop Trail narrows significantly. After crossing the fall's branch on a footbridge, the trail winds, climbs, and then parallels the creek that feeds the spout-type waterfall mentioned in the text of the Keown Falls Loop Trail. At just over a mile, cross this creek. The trail climbs at a moderate rate out of the creek bottom then turns right at the base of a ridge. Heading south along the east side of the ridge, at 1.25 miles the trail veers right to tread its crest. The larger boulders in this area are covered in toadskin lichen. At 1.3 miles the rocky treadway gives way to woodland humus. It may go unnoticed but at 1.55 miles the trail is now at its apex and with gradual right turns begins heading for the parking area. The trail now twists and turns west over a high point between hollows both north and south. At 1.7 miles the trail turns north to parallel the west side of Johns Mountain's north-south ridgeline. The rock outcrops again return and increase in frequency. Many times the trail treads over small boulders and bedrock. At 2.4 miles the trail begins to ascend at an easy rate changing to a more moderate rate nearing the trail's end. Pass a radio tower and transmission building then at 3.1 miles arrive back at the parking area.

Cohutta Wilderness Area

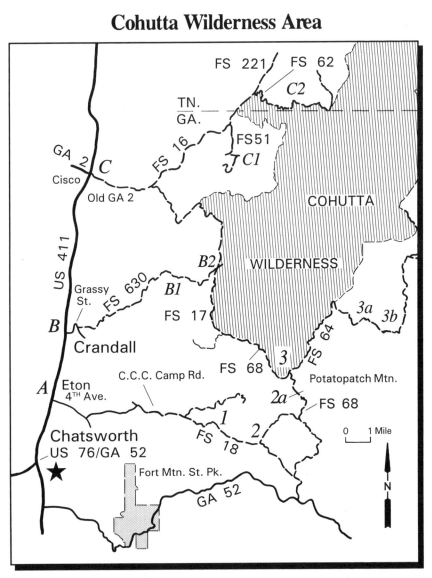

Directions: From the intersection of U.S. 76/Ga. 52 and U.S. 411 in Chatsworth, drive north on 411 to access the following points of interest:

A. 4TH Ave. in Eton, access to the Falls on Emery Creek, the Falls on Barnes Creek, the Falls on Crenshaw Branch (Mountaintown Creek drainage), and the Falls on the South Fork Jacks River: 2.8 miles.

B. Grassy St. in Crandall, access to Mill and Panther Creek Falls: 6.0 miles. Text for "B" begins on pg. 17.

C. Old Ga. Hwy. 2, access to the Falls on Jiggers Creek and Jacks River Falls: 12.05 miles. Text for "C" begins on pg. 21.

A. Directions: From U.S. 411 in Eton, drive east on 4ᵀᴴ Ave. (The Eton branch of the First National Bank of Chatsworth is located at the southeast corner of this intersection. This road changes into C.C.C. Camp Road and splits left in 1.5 miles. Continuing, at 6.2 miles the road's designation changes to F.S. 18 and the pavement ends upon entry into the National Forest.) From 411, drive the distances listed below to the following points of interest:

1. Parking for the Emery Creek Trail: 7.45 miles.
2. The intersection of F.S. 68: 10.35 miles. Access to: (2a) the Falls on Barnes Creek and (3) Potatopatch Mountain (see directions pg. 15).

1. Falls on Emery Creek, Emery Creek Trail, Murray County, Georgia

Roads: Graveled   An "8"
U.S.G.S. Quadrangle: Crandall, Ga.
Trail #97, 2.2 miles to falls, 3.15 miles to trail's end, water crossings, moderate

At this location look for the parking area on the left side of F.S. 18 at the beginning of a sharp right bend.

The trail to Emery Creek Falls begins at the northeast end of the parking area behind the information board.

Pass between the wooden guardrails and enter the woods over jeep-blocking mounds. The trail immediately turns uphill then tops out at 600'. Before it descends, look for and take a steep side path leading down to a view of Holly Creek's cascades and swirlholes.

Back on the main trail, at .2 of a mile arrive alongside Holly Creek whose boulders have been polished smooth by water-borne sediments. The trail becomes very rocky here. At the quarter-mile point, just above the confluence of Emery Creek, cross Holly Creek. In another 150' cross to Emery Creek's west side. At .4 of a mile cross to the east bank of Emery Creek. At .45 of a mile, trail and creek bend right. For the next .2 of a mile you leave sight of the creek. Though turning slightly uphill, the trail becomes easier as it treads a logging road. Three quarters of a mile into the hike cross to the left (now north) side of the creek. In this and many spots along the Emery Creek Trail you hike under a canopy of rhododendron. At .9 of a mile pass the juncture of Bear Branch which joins on the right. Amongst the windfalls, the treadway becomes very rocky around the 1 mile point and soon crosses to the right side of the creek. In the creek bottom look for signs of rooting done by wild hogs. In the next .2 of a mile pass a long-abandoned truck then cross to the left side of Emery Creek below the entry of an unnamed creek. In 115' (1.2 miles into the hike) intersect a graveled road (F.S. 78C). (This is accessed from the Tibbs ORV Trail which is closed to automobile traffic.)

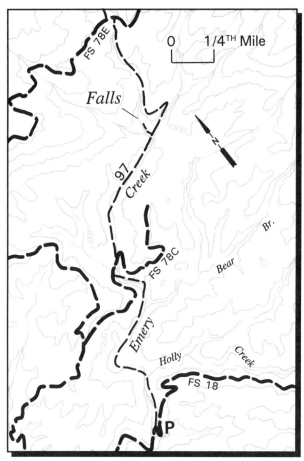

Hike 78C east, immediately crossing a stream. The road parallels Emery Creek for .15 of a mile then descends to ford it. Preceding this *second* ford, at a "Closed to Vehicles" sign, reenter the woods and hike upstream on the Emery Creek Trail. The trail climbs steeply for 300' then levels off on an old roadbed which now serves as the trail. Nearing the creek, again the trail becomes rockier, then at 1.65 miles crosses to Emery Creek's right (east) side followed by the next crossing in .1 of a mile to the west side. Soon the trail starts uphill. It then eases slightly to make a more gradual ascent. At 2.15 miles cross to the right side of Emery Creek at its confluence with an unnamed creek. The trail turns steeply uphill here and in less than 100' arrives at the spur trail, on the left, leading to Emery Creek Falls. (The Emery Creek Trail continues straight ahead.) Take the spur upstream for 375' to the base of the falls.

Seen from a large boulder on a midstream island, this beautiful waterfall cascades 25' and runs 30' spilling into a triangular-shaped plunge pool which is narrowed at the downstream end. During my visit alot of driftwood had snagged on this island. Steep, hardwood-covered hillsides flank both the left and right sides of the creek. Emery Creek's clear waters exit the pool over flat, rounded stones.

Back on the Emery Creek Trail, continue upstream along the unnamed creek. The trail is now much steeper as are the hemlock-covered mountainsides. At just over 2.3 miles the roadbed serving as the trail turns sharply left, leaving the unnamed creek. At 2.45 miles the trail begins making a long bend north where the distant sounds of Emery Creek return. At 2.65 miles a succession of three small waterfalls begins. They may be seen through the trees or by hiking downstream via a slim pathway near the stream crossing that lies just ahead.

Crossing to the creek's west side, at 2.75 miles the trail runs through an overflow area for a short distance. From this point the trail makes two more crossings, then at 3.15 miles, amongst the poison ivy, arrives at F.S. 78E (the end of our hike). A less traveled section of the Emery Creek Trail offsets 110' to the northwest here, treading F.S. 78E before reentering the woods.

2. Directions: From the intersection of F.S. Roads 18 and 68, drive north on 68 to the following locations:

2(a) The Falls on Barnes Creek: 3.6 miles.

3. Potatopatch Mountain, the intersection of F.S. 68 and 64: 5.9 miles. Access to: 3(a) the Falls on Crenshaw Branch and 3(b) the Falls on the South Fork Jacks River (see below).

2(a) Falls on Barnes Creek,
Gilmer County, Georgia

Roads: Graveled   A "3" 15'
U.S.G.S. Quadrangle: Dyer Gap, Ga.
Easy   Adjacent to road.

The parking area for the Barnes Creek Picnic Area is located on the right side of F.S. 68.

This is a great spot for fine outdoor dining, then to walk it off while exploring the falls.

From the picnic area a pathway and steps on the left lead 200' to the observation deck atop the falls. The most enjoyable view of this waterfall, however, is while cooling your feet in the shallow waters of its base.

This waterfall is very scenic after adequate rainfall. The rock face splits its flow into two streams. Being high in the drainage area, in the dry months they're a mere trickle.

In summer the left side receives a great deal of sunlight while the right side is deeply shaded. This harsh lighting makes for tricky photographic conditions.

3. Directions: From the intersection of F.S. Roads 68 and 64, on Potatopatch Mountain, drive east on 64 to access these points of interest:

3(a) The Mountaintown Creek parking area and trailhead (Falls on Crenshaw Branch): 7.0 miles.

3(b) Trail parking for the South Fork Jacks River Trail: 8.9 miles.

3(a) Falls on Crenshaw Br., Mountaintown Cr. Trail, Fannin and Gilmer Counties, Georgia

Roads: Graveled   A "4"
U.S.G.S. Quadrangle: Dyer Gap, Ga.
Trail #135, orange blazed, water crossings, difficult

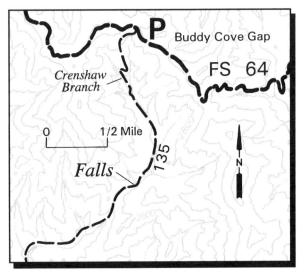

From the parking area at Buddy Cove Gap, this hiking/mountain bike trail descends steeply via an old logging road. At the outset this woodland treadway is made slim as it passes through knee-high growth. Paralleling the east side of a ridge, in approximately .3 of a mile the trail levels and soon bends right to round the base of that ridge. At .55 of a mile arrive at a sharp left bend. Here you'll join Crenshaw Branch, which for the time being is on the trail's west side. I found a tattered sign here stating "Mountaintown Creek artificial lures only." Continuing downstream, at .75 of a mile cross to the west side of Crenshaw Branch. In this area you'll sometimes be in open woods and at others under a canopy of laurel. On the trailside lie thick patches of club and haircap mosses. At 1.2 miles cross to the east side of the creek. In another .1 of a mile a tributary joins from the east and runs alongside the trail. Soon you'll cross to the west side Crenshaw Branch just above its confluence with this tributary. At 1.6 miles cross to the east bank and in 300' top a small rise. You can hear the rushing creek below. The trail descends while treading over a rocky and wet stretch. At 1.7 miles arrive at a point where the falls are viewed from the side.

This is a sliding-type waterfall with several breaks. Its width increases as it falls, from 12' at the top to 20' at the base.

Trees native to the area are, American holly, beech, Fraser magnolia, hemlock, maple, and poplar.

This rugged trail continues for approximately 4.0 additional miles and ties into F.S. 241.

3(b) Falls on the South Fork Jacks River, Fannin County, Georgia

Roads: Graveled   A "4" & "5" respectively
U.S.G.S. Quadrangle: Dyer Gap, Ga.
Trail #140, .3 of a mile, easy

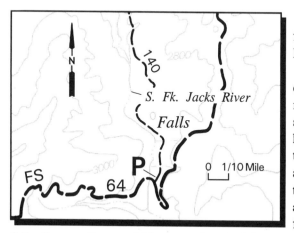

At this location look for trail parking on the left.

As you enter the woods cross two jeep-blocking mounds and pass a sign stating "Closed to vehicles." The trail crosses two wet-weather branches and outlines their hollows, then in .3 of a mile arrives at a point where the upper falls are heard. Look carefully for a pathway which turns sharply left then back to the right while descending to the base area 70' away.

This pockmarked waterfall is not large (10-12'), but it does have a great deal of power. Rhododendron limbs thrust themselves out over its turbulent plunge pool to naturally frame the setting.

To reach the lower falls, return towards the main trail and hike downstream approximately 200' on an exploratory pathway to this 6' sliding-type waterfall. Rhododendron overhangs the banks of its colorful plunge pool, setting off the soft browns, golds, and whites of the stones in its blue-green waters.

B. Directions: As you turn east onto Grassy St. from U.S. 411 in Crandall, zero your odometer. In .4 of a mile cross the CSX Railroad tracks then turn right onto Crandall - Ellijay Road. In another .1 of a mile turn left onto F.S. 630 (Mill Creek Road). Drive the following distances from U.S. 411 to access the points listed below:

B1. Hickey Gap, access to Mill Creek Falls: 7.3 miles.
B2. The intersection of F.S. 17: 9.6 miles. Cross this intersection and drive .25 of a mile to the parking area and trailhead for the Hickory Creek Trail, and Panther Creek Falls.

B1. Mill Creek Falls,
Murray County, Georgia

Roads: Graveled   A "3"   No hiking map needed.
U.S.G.S. Quadrangle: Tennga, Ga., Tenn.
No official trail, .1 of a mile, easy

Directions: Turn right and descend the steep road. In less than .1 of a mile arrive at the parking area. The pathway to the falls begins at large in-ground boulders on the downstream end of the parking area.

From the boulders the pathway enters a rhododendron thicket that gives way to laurel. Notice the interesting bedrock underfoot with quartz intermixed. At 290' the pathway turns right to circumvent the falls. Alongside them the rooty pathway is protected by railing. Soon the pathway descends steeply and at .1 of a mile arrives at the fall's midpoint.

This 30' cascading waterfall runs for 200' in a long, lazy S. The midpoint boulders are just right for sunning and drinking in the beautiful sights.

The pathway continues downstream for another 140' to the base. From this point swirlholes are visible as is the crisscross striping of quartz veins.

B2. Panther Creek Falls,
Fannin County, Georgia

Roads: Graveled   A "6"
Map: The Cohutta Wilderness
Trail #'s 10, white blazed; 11, yellow blazed; 116, blue blazed, 4.75 miles, water crossings, difficult

Note: I saw my first wild hogs while returning from this backcountry location.

I first visited the falls on a summer day in 1990. Being high in Panther Creek's drainage and a dry time of the year to boot, there wasn't much water. Still, I came away very impressed with the rock face and its beautiful colors. To see them at their best go after rainfall, but be careful of the potentially deep Conasauga River crossing.

The Hickory Creek Trail (#10) enters the woods near the information board on the east side of the parking lot at a gate with a sign stating "Road Closed." Descending initially over a rocky stretch, soon pass the trail register. At times the roadbed serving as the trail is easily walked then at others very rocky and difficult. At 625' cross a small branch and outline the other side of its hollow with a slight uphill climb. The trail begins to descend at a moderate rate then at .55 of a mile makes a hard right and continues its descent, soon crossing another small branch.

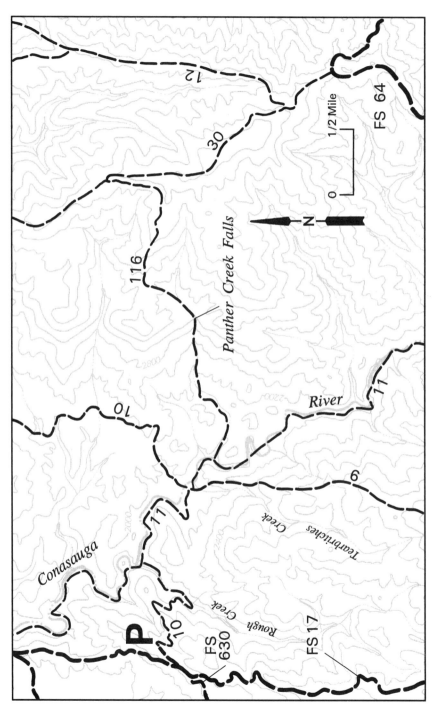

On this higher ground the trail passes through hardwoods with sweetshrub thickly filling the understory voids. In spring, this small tree-like shrub has dozens of deep maroon-brown colored blooms whose loosely arranged petals resemble silk flowers. In this and other woodland locations chipmunks sound the alarm. With a shrill cross between a bird chirp and squeak toy-like ...sssweet!, they alert their neighbors to your presence.

With a slight right turn, at .85 of a mile the rushing waters of Rough Creek can be heard on the left. At 1.05 miles the trail turns sharply left at a small branch that immediately joins a larger creek. The trail now parallels Rough Creek north and east. Rhododendron grows thick on the slopes of this wetter microclimate. At 1.35 miles cross a small creek on steppingstones. The trail outlines the remainder of its cove and treads over a rocky wet stretch, within a stone's throw of Rough Creek. At 1.55 miles the trail becomes even rockier while treading through Rough Creek's overflow area. Rough Creek is soon crossed on steppingstones.

One and sixty-five hundredths miles into the hike, pass by a popular camping area at the confluence of Rough Creek and the Conasauga River. The Hickory Creek and Conasauga River Trails intersect here as well. Hike upstream on #11 the Conasauga River/Hickory Creek Trail. Initially, this combined trail has wet stretches and is a bit on the rocky side, but the beauty of the river outweighs any physical difficulties presented. At 1.85 miles the trail ascends, bends in conjunction with the river, then descends back to river level. At 2.3 miles the trail and river turn southwest and soon thereafter, with a slight rise, tread alongside a huge and very scenic beaver pond (depending on whether the dams hold). This is a great place for fall foliage shots with trees and sky mirrored in the still waters.

In .2 of a mile the trail turns towards the woods and away from the beaver pond while leading uphill. Upon reentering the woods cross a small branch flowing through a concrete pipe. After topping out, the trail dips to cross a small wet-weather branch in a vale filled with ferns. The trail then rises again and bends slightly right, winding and dipping through the woods in unison with the old roadbed. At 2.85 miles pass under a canopy of laurel and cross a small wet-weather branch, then enter a grassy meadow. While crossing this meadow, look for a road cut that leads to the river bank. The Hickory Creek Trail splits left to ford the river, parting with the Conasauga River Trail. Continuing on the Conasauga River Trail (on the right), in just over 200', as the trail reenters the woods, pass the Tearbritches Trail (#9) which begins on the right.

Now plying the woods on its own, at 3.05 miles the Conasauga River Trail crosses Tearbritches Creek. The trail immediately climbs out of the creek bottom and in .1 of a mile tops a ridge line, undulates, then descends to river level. (In this area, on the official map, the Conasauga River Trail is shown incorrectly as being on the east side of the river.) At 3.45 miles arrive at the intersection of the Panther Creek Trail (#116). This trail junction is just upstream from a prominent riverside camping area. (Just downstream from this camping area is a very scenic stretch of river.) The Conasauga River Trail continues upstream, while the Panther Creek Trail leads immediately to the river and crosses just above the confluence of their namesakes.

Cross the river (at times knee-deep) and enter the Panther Creek drainage. The trail closely follows the creek, crossing then recrossing it many times. While climbing at a moderate to difficult rate, at 4.2 miles the trail leaves the creekside for the drier slopes of the hardwood forest. The trail becomes rockier and more boulder strewn at 4.5 miles as it dips to cross the now very scenic Panther Creek. For the next .25 of a mile the trail is even more difficult as it climbs the cove over rubble. Unless freshly blazed, the route is often hard to follow as the rock shows no track. Finally, at 4.75 miles cross a fallen hemlock trunk to access the falls. (The Panther Creek Trail continues steeply up the cove and ties into the East Cowpen Trail in approximately 1.5 miles.)

Panther Creek falls a total of 45' in two tiers over a 30'-wide rock face. The split-stream upper tier falls 25'. The majority of the creek's flow is over the left side. At times the right side may be dry. The lower tier slides for 10' then cascades the remaining 10'.

This location photographs best under diffused lighting.

C. Directions: From U.S. 411 in Cisco, where Ga. Hwy. 2 turns west, turn right (east) onto Old Hwy. 2 (the Cisco Baptist Church is located at the northeast corner of this intersection). This road changes to F.S. 16 as it enters the National Forest. Its designation changes to F.S. 221 as it enters Tennessee. From Hwy. 411 drive the following distances to these points of interest:

C1. F.S. 51, access to the Falls on Jiggers Creek: 7.9 miles.

C2. F.S. 62, access to Jacks River Falls: 9.8 miles.

C1. Falls on Jiggers Creek,
Murray County, Georgia

Roads: Graveled   A "2"
U.S.G.S. Quadrangle: Tennga, Ga., Tenn.
May be seen from car.

Note: Best seen after rainfall.

Directions: From F.S. 16 take F.S. 51 (a steep, single-lane graveled road) for 1.6 miles to the pullouts which double as the parking area and turnaround.

Another turnaround is located at the Horseshoe Bend Trail parking area just ahead (if you can ford the often deep creek en route to it).

This waterfall may be seen from the side of the road or from a path that leads to its base. To reach the base, pace off a distance of 35' from the point where they're viewed from the road. Here you'll find a steep pathway leading down to the pool area.

Be very careful on the slick rocks in and around the creek.

The falls are broken into three cascades with a total drop of 15'. The rock wall on the right is adorned with mosses, lichens, and aquatic plants, with hemlock and maple atop it.

C2. Jacks River Falls, Fannin County, Georgia

Roads: Graveled   A "10"
Map: The Cohutta Wilderness
Trail #'s 74 ; 13, orange blazed, 4.6 miles, water crossings, moderate

---

Directions: From F.S. 221 turn sharply right onto F.S. 62 and drive 4.6 miles to the parking area for #74 the Beech Bottom Trail (trail to the falls) on the left. The trail begins at the information board on the east side of F.S. 62.

The trail (an old roadbed) is flat and level initially and outlines the hillsides much like a contour line. Pass the trail register, then at one third of a mile enter the Georgia portion of the Cohutta Wilderness. The trail begins making a more obvious descent here. This dry, higher ground is covered in hardwoods and pine with pinxter azalea here and there. The noble pileated woodpecker calls this woodland sanctuary home and makes its presence known to intruders. On the lower slopes you'll encounter laurels, rhododendron, hemlock, and beech trees. At the half-mile point the trail makes an even more noticeable descent. At 1 mile the rush of an unnamed stream accompanies your descent. Soon the trail dips to cross a tributary then follows the main stream uphill. This hollow has huge poplar and hemlock, but of special note are gigantic beech trees some of which are 3' in diameter. In this more moist environment are, crested dwarf iris, foamflower, galax, trillium, and wild geranium. The trail climbs at a moderate rate along this small creek. At 1.35 miles the trail turns right as it crosses this creek which flows under the roadbed through a culvert.

Climbing out of this lowland at a moderate rate, the trail leaves earshot of the creek as you round a left bend. At 1.65 miles the trail levels while rounding a high point. Running level for the next .4 of a mile the trail then turns slightly uphill. On a ridge line high above its hollow, the trail parallels the unnamed creek crossed at 1.35 miles. At 2.4 miles pass through a small gap. As the trail turns downhill the distant sounds of Jacks River are heard. In the next half mile outline five successive hollows of varying depth.

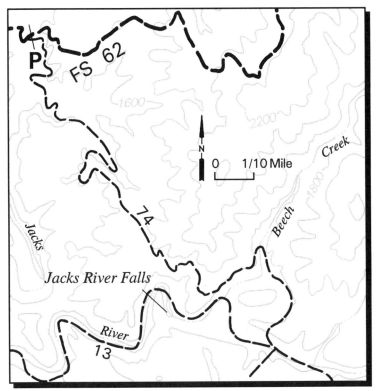

At 2.9 miles enter the roadbed's noticeably deeper cut in which the trail turns sharply left. In this area while descending into the Beech Creek drainage you can see beautiful mountains to the east and south and hear Jacks River Falls as well. Seen from left to right are: Hemp Top, Dally Gap, the Jacks River Valley, and Hickory Ridge which lies due south. At 3.2 miles, while descending, the trail bends left and Beech Creek comes into view below. After passing a primitive camping area the trail crosses Beech Creek at 3.4 miles on steppingstones (possibly a wet crossing). On the creek's east side tread through the rocky overflow area. During high water I'm sure this section of trail would be under water.

At 3.45 miles, back on higher ground and out of the rock, the trail veers left and away from the creek as it outlines the base of a mountain in open woods. There is evidence of an old homestead here: fence, washtubs, rock piles, etc. The trail soon reenters deeper woods and crosses a couple of small branches. Ascending slightly from Beech Creek, at 3.9 miles top a rise while bending left. From this point the trail descends, passes through a primitive camping area, then at 4.05 miles arrives at a riverside juncture with #13 the Jacks River Trail. The Hickory Ridge Trail (shown incorrectly on the official map) lies 130' east of this intersection.

Take the Jacks River Trail downstream. After running level for .2 of a mile, the trail descends an easy rate and soon passes several rock outcrops while bending in unison with the deceivingly placid river. At 4.4 miles the river makes a noticeable bend left and the trail crosses a small branch. At its confluence with Jacks River (4.5 miles), cross Beech Creek on steppingstones (downstream from a popular camping area). As you cross Beech Creek the prelude to Jacks River Falls is seen downstream. Between Beech Creek and the falls (just under .2 of a mile) the trail is especially rocky, treading through the river's overflow area.

The 8' upper tier falls into a large pool in an open bedrock area. As you approach its pool look for two large drill bits sticking up out of the bedrock on the left side. The river has carved swirlholes in the bedrock. After a slight pause, the churning and more scenic lower tier tumbles over its rock face. Together the falls run for 200' and lose 60' in elevation, in a rugged setting of exposed rock flanked by hemlock, and white and scrub pines.

This waterfall photographs best under bright sunny conditions when its great power is best captured.

Dahlonega West

Amicalola Falls State Park, Dawson County, Georgia

Roads: Paved   A "10" Ga. fee area
U.S.G.S. Quadrangle: Amicalola, Nimblewill, Ga.
Trails range from very easy to difficult (see table below).

The park's great beauty and close proximity to the metro Atlanta area make it one of north Georgia's most popular attractions. Spotlessly clean, the park boasts 1020 acres, fine dining, a 57 room lodge, 14 cottages, and its main attraction: the state's highest waterfall, Amicalola Falls, which falls and cascades for a total of 729'. The park is also the beginning point for the 8 mile approach trail to the southern terminus of the Appalachian Trail located on Springer Mountain.

It seems that most of the park's patrons stay close to the car and visit only the falls. In spite of the park's heavy visitation there are still trails (3.25 miles of them) where quiet time is easily found. Deer and squirrel are frequently seen along these trails. Two of my favorite spots are a view of the falls from the West Ridge Spring Trail and the view of the mountains to the south from the East Ridge Spring Trail. Distances for the park's trails are listed below.

Directions: From the intersection of Ga. Hwys. 9 and 52 (approximately 4 miles west of Dahlonega), take Hwy. 52 west approximately 14 miles to the park's entrance (Amicalola Falls State Park Road). The visitor center is .3 of a mile ahead.

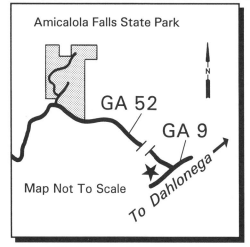

Top of the Falls: Directly across from the visitor center, Top of the Falls Road winds steeply up the mountainside for 1.2 miles to the parking area for its namesake (and then continues onward to the lodge).

A paved trail leads 250' to the overlook. From atop Amicalola Falls, spectacular views are to be had of the distant mountains to the south. This is an excellent spot for autumn leaf shots.

Base of Falls Trail: From the visitor center continue straight ahead (north) for .4 of a mile to the parking area and trailhead.

From the parking area the paved trail passes the reflection pool and in 260' crosses Little Amicalola Creek on a footbridge. Trailside plaques tell of local flora and fauna. Some of the plants found here include toadshade trillium, foamflower,

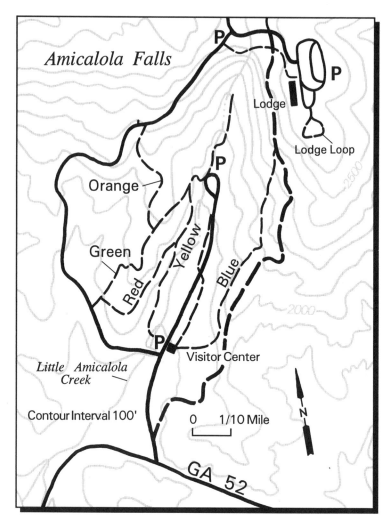

Amicalola Falls

Lodge

Lodge Loop

Orange

Green

Red

Yellow

Blue

P

Visitor Center

Little Amicalola Creek

Contour Interval 100'

0   1/10 Mile

N

GA 52

Mayapple, Solomon's seal, and an occasional flame azalea. At 500' the trail parallels the creek and climbs steeply. At .2 of a mile the trail turns right to switchback up the hillside. Arrive at the fall's observation deck at .3 of a mile.

West Ridge Spring Trail (Orange) moderate .... .35 of a mile

Upper West Ridge Trail (Green) moderate .... .49 of a mile

Lower West Ridge Trail (Red) easy-moderate .... .19 of a mile

Creek Trail (Yellow) moderate-difficult .... .52 of a mile

Base of Falls Trail (Paved) moderate-difficult .... .29 of a mile

East Ridge Spring Trail (Blue) moderate-difficult .... 1.15 miles

Lodge Loop Trail (wheelchair accessible) very easy ... .25 of a mile

Dahlonega North

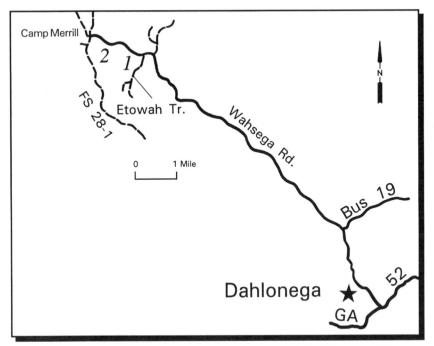

Directions: From the Gold Museum, on the square in Dahlonega, drive east for .1 of a mile to Bus. 19/60. Turn left and travel 2.25 miles to Wahsega Road (sign: "Camp Frank D. Merrill"). Turn left and drive the following distances to these points of interest. All locations listed below are in Lumpkin County, unless otherwise noted.

1. Etowah Trail (a lightly graveled road), access to Edmunston Falls: 7.25 miles.
2. F.S. 28-1, access to Black Falls: 8.6 miles. (The main gate for Camp Merrill is located at this intersection.)

1. Edmunston Falls

Roads: Dirt   A "2"   20'   No hiking map needed.
U.S.G.S. Quadrangle: Campbell Mtn., Ga.
No official trail, .2 of a mile, water crossing, easy

Note: The dirt road mentioned below may be impassable after rainfall.
Directions: At this location turn left onto Etowah Trail and drive south for .5 of mile to an unmarked dirt road and turn right. In approximately 200' cross the fall's creek which flows through a culvert. Park in a small pullout on the right,

just before the road bends left (less than .1 of a mile from Etowah Trail).

Hike the road downstream for just over .1 of a mile passing by the falls which are seen and heard on the left. Look for an obvious wide spot in the road and pace off 120'. Descend the steep bank to creek level. Cross the creek and hike upstream through the open woods for 250' to the base area.

This waterfall has suffered storm damage and has fallen trees veiling much of its beauty. In time these windfalls will be broken down by insects, fungi, and mosses and returned to the earth in life's continuing process.

2. Black Falls

Roads: Graveled   A "5" 15'
U.S.G.S. Quadrangle: Campbell Mtn., Ga.
No official trail, .25 of a mile, moderate

Note: Normally, this would be an easy hike. Granted, the logging road serving as the trail *is* a steep one, but the short distance to the falls makes up for that. Storms have been both beneficial and detrimental to this spot. Beneficial in that several trees blocking the view have been eliminated. On the minus side are the many windfalls that must be crossed over and ducked under en route to the falls. Hopefully you'll find the roadbed cleared for much easier hiking.

Camp Merrill   (Off Limits)
Contour Interval 20'

0   1/10 Mile
N

Black Creek —

Falls —

FS 28-1

P

Directions: At this location turn left onto F.S. 28-1. Pass by the Mt. Zion Church, on the left, and soon thereafter the army camp's gym, on the right. In .5 of a mile arrive at the parking area on the right. There are three possible parking choices here. Use the road in the middle, which also serves as the pathway to the falls, or the road to the left of it. The road on the extreme right, with the triangular-shaped guardrail, leads down to Camp Merrill and is *off limits*.

Upon entering the woods the roadbed is level for 150' then bends left while descending the western slope of the mountain. At 650' encounter the first of the aforementioned windfalls. At just over .2 of a mile arrive alongside, but high above, a shoaling Black Creek. Seen in this vicinity are large hemlock, white pine, and sweetgum. The road bottoms out then bends right as it passes beds of galax and more windfalls. At .25 of a mile, arrive at a point where the falls are seen from the road. To see them from the base, work your way over the tops of downed trees to a sandy viewing area at creek level.

Stonepile Gap Area

Stonepile Gap is the legendary gravesite of Cherokee Princess, Trahlyta. As her people and early settlers passed through, they would lay stones on her grave in remembrance, thus the name Stonepile Gap. Today U.S. 19 and Ga. Hwy. 60 intersect here. This intersection is approximately 9.1 miles north of Dahlonega. This is the beginning point for the routes listed below.

The following waterfalls are located in Lumpkin County, unless otherwise noted.

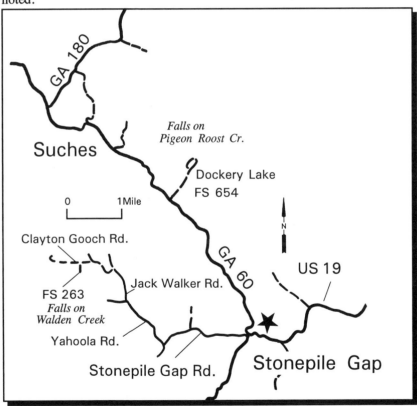

Falls on Walden Creek

Roads: Graveled A "4"
U.S.G.S. Quadrangle: Suches, Ga.
No official trail, 1.3 miles, moderate

Note: Many of the road signs en route to the falls were missing or arranged in a confusing manner, please pay careful attention to the driving directions below.

Directions: From U.S. 19 at Stonepile Gap, drive west on Stonepile Gap Road (sign: "R-Ranch"). Pass through R-Ranch Resort and in 1.9 miles arrive at a stop sign intersection with Yahoola Road. Turn right and travel 1.5 miles to Jack Walker Road. Again, turn right. In .4 of a mile bear left. Jack Walker Road soon turns steeply uphill. After driving 1 mile from Yahoola Road turn left onto Clayton Gooch Road. In .2 of a mile, where the roadway starts steeply uphill, look for the gated F.S. 263 which is on the left. Park so as to not block the gate. The hike begins at the gate.

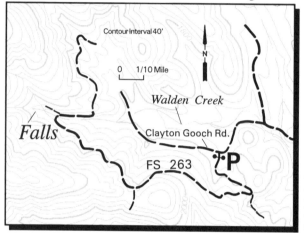

Hike the winding, lightly graveled F.S. 263. In one-quarter mile the road makes a hard right. There is a potentially confusing pathway on the left here. Continue on the wide and open roadbed on the right as it outlines the mountainside and ascends at a moderate rate. The forest along the roadbed to Walden Creek is primarily hardwood. In spots the route is thickly lined with laurel with galax. The orange of flame azalea dotting the mountainsides immediately catches one's eye in stark contrast to the mute colors of early spring.

At .75 of a mile pass a pathway on the left that leads into the woods to shortcut a saddle ridge. This is the highest point of the hike. The roadbed now descends while outlining the mountainside. At 1.25 miles the roadbed bends sharply right while crossing the culvert through which Walden Creek flows. (This is the first substantial creek that you will encounter.) After crossing, enter the woods on a pathway leading up the creek's north side. Hike this pathway for 320' to the fall's viewing area. The falls are seen approximately 70' away.

Entering the scene as a cascade, this unspoiled beauty makes a sheer 12' drop, showering the rock below. The creek then flows through rock and driftwood towards the viewing area where it is joined by a creek from the right.

There is a waterfall up this neighboring creek as well. It is located approximately 200' from the viewing area of the Falls on Walden Creek. This shoaling, white-water slide is approximately 15' high and must be seen from a distance because of the cove's steepness.

The Falls on Walden Creek photograph best on an overcast day or in the early morning before the sun filters through the canopy. Late afternoon is also a good time with the sun hidden behind the mountain.

Lakeshore Trail and Falls, Dockery Lake Rec. Area

Roads: Graveled   A "2"
U.S.G.S. Quadrangle: Neels Gap, Ga.
Loop trail .55 of a mile, Falls: see text, easy-moderate

Directions: From Stonepile Gap, drive north on Hwy. 60 for 3.75 miles to Dockery Lake Road (F.S. 654). Turn right onto this graveled road and travel 1 mile to the picnic area access road. Turn left and in .4 of a mile arrive at the parking area and trailhead. (Also see the Falls on Pigeon Roost Creek pg. 32.)

Along this shoreline hike are openings to cast a line or for viewing this beautiful high-country lake. In the spring Dockery Lake is stocked with trout until its shallow waters become too warm (75°) for them to survive. Fall is a great time

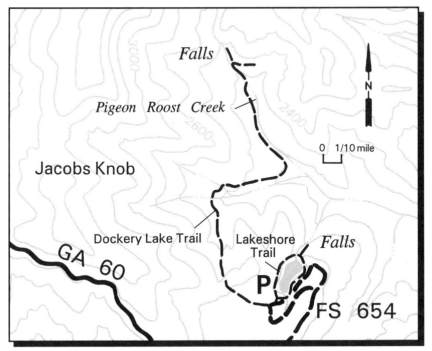

to visit for colorful foliage and blue skies reflected in its waters. With a surface area of approximately six acres, the lake is too small for powerboating. Boats with trolling motors or man-powered craft *are* allowed.

Enter the woods at the *north* end of the parking area. Descending at a moderate

rate, pass through the picnic area and in 400′ intersect the loop trail. Directions given for this loop are clockwise.

Cross a small creek via a footbridge and hike the level shoreline through a forest of hemlock, maple, oak, poplar, and white pine. Just shy of .3 of a mile arrive at a footbridge over the spillway. On the east side of this bridge is an exploratory path leading downstream to a cascading waterfall.

To reach the falls, wiggle your way through the laurel on this barely discernable path for approximately 400′ to a bedrock exposure. With your hands free, continue down the slim pathway for another 150′ to a viewing area beside the falls.

In this vicinity, notice a poplar blown over in its youth that now grows horizontally for 15′ before turning skyward. This is one aspect of a natural forest that I like—there are no cookie-cutter look-alikes. Each tree has a well-defined personality.

Return to the Lakeshore Trail and hike the east portion of the loop. The trail now passes by the campground and its picnic areas. Nearing the half-mile point, pass a rock wall and then cross a sandy-bottomed creek on another footbridge. Duck boxes set among the reeds of the shallow mud flats make this the more scenic end of the lake. At .55 of a mile tie back into the beginning of the loop.

Falls on Pigeon Roost Creek, Dockery Lake Trail

U.S.G.S. Quadrangle: Neels Gap, Ga.   A "4"
Blue blazed, 1.95 miles, water crossings,
moderate-difficult   Shares Lakeshore Trail and Falls map.

Note: Best seen after rainfall.

Directions: Same as Lakeshore Trail (above). The trail to the falls begins on the *west* side of the parking area at a sign stating: "Dockery Lake Trail, Miller Gap 3, Appalachian Trail 3."

For the first .2 of a mile the trail climbs at a moderate rate. It then becomes easier, allowing for a non-stop chance to catch your breath. At .3 of a mile pass over the ridge through a saddle-type gap. (From this point, the old logging road [trail] descends, often steeply, for the next .9 of a mile to Pigeon Roost Creek.)

At .45 of a mile pass large sandstone boulders and a scattering of milky quartz. At .55 of a mile an old overgrown road (shown on the quadrangle) takes off to the right—blink your eyes and you'll miss it. Just ahead cross a small but scenic boulder-strewn creek. Cross two more small creeks draining off Jacobs Knob; the first at .85 of a mile, and the second at .9 of a mile. Between the two of them are informal camping areas in the open woods.

Continuing down the mountainside, the trail now parallels (at a distance) a rushing and cascading Jacobs Knob Branch (formed by the three previously crossed tributaries). Nearing the bottom of the slope the trail crosses a wet-weather branch which then spills onto the trail as well. One and two-tenths miles into the hike, enter an area of storm damage as you turn up Pigeon Roost Creek's cove. At 1.3 miles cross a wet-weather branch and the trail starts uphill, soon rounding a left bend. (From this point to the falls the trail climbs at a moderate rate.) Through the open woods the creek may be seen on the right. Nearing 1.5 miles enter a stretch of moss-covered rock banked four-feet high on both sides of the trail. At 1.55 miles cross a small branch on steppingstones. The trail continues its ascent and bends sharply left. At 1.75 miles, cross beautiful boulder-strewn Pigeon Roost Creek. The creek and trail soon run close together with more great views of this magnificent creek.

At 1.9 miles the road which serves as the trail turns sharply right and steeply uphill (and eventually ties into the Appalachian Trail at Miller Gap). Let your eyes follow the creek up the cove, where it then disappears behind boulders 250' ahead. Leave the main trail here and parallel the creek up this cove at a distance of 50'. (You may be able to detect an overgrown logging road on the north side to use as a pathway.) As you venture up the steepening cove, the creek makes the transition from cascades over boulders to slides over bedrock and soon thereafter the falls. At 1.95 miles arrive at the spot where the small double falls are viewed.

The falls on the left are 20' high. Those on the right are 15' high and have more water volume. Both fall in 3 to 5' stairsteps.

Vasey's trillium, ferns, hemlock, giant poplar, oaks, and hickory are found up their cove.

Suches Area

Directions: From the intersection of Georgia Hwys. 60 and 180 in Suches, take Hwy. 60 north to the following points of interest. The falls listed under this heading are located in Fannin County, Georgia.

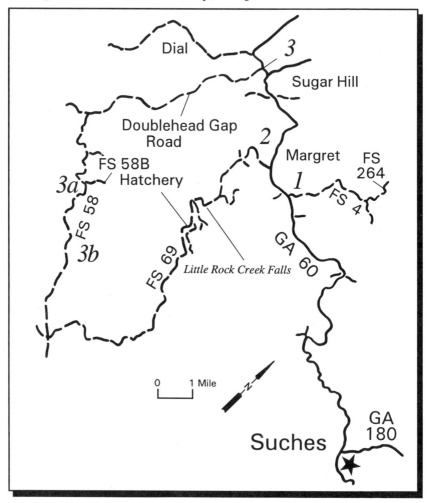

1. F.S. 4, access to Sea Creek Falls: approximately 11 miles.
2. F.S. 69, access to Little Rock Creek Falls: approximately 12 miles.
3. Doublehead Gap Road, access to (a) Noontootla and (b) Long Creek Falls: approximately 15.75 miles.

1. Sea Creek Falls

Roads: Graveled   A "4" 25'
U.S.G.S. Quadrangle: Mulky Gap, Ga.
No official trail, easy

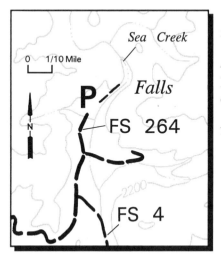

Note: F.S. 264 may have deep mudholes after rainfall.

Directions: From Hwy. 60 take F.S. 4 east for 3.0 miles to F.S. 264. Turn left and drive .3 of a mile to a primitive campground and the base of the falls.

Sea Creek cascades into a large and beautiful pool in an alpine setting.

2. Little Rock Creek Falls

Roads: Graveled   An "8" 20'
U.S.G.S. Quadrangle: Noontootla, Ga.
No official trail, .45 of a mile, minor water crossings, moderate

Directions: From the intersection of F.S. 69 and Hwy. 60 (sign: "Chattahoochee National Fish Hatchery"), take F.S. 69 for 3.35 miles to a bridge that

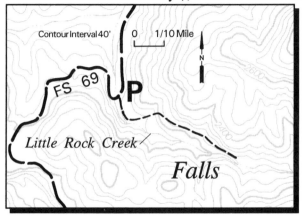

crosses Little Rock Creek in a sharp bend to the right. Park here.

Since my first visit to this waterfall, in 1990, there has been storm damage. This has altered the hiking route and made the falls a little harder to reach. In addition, the falls viewing area has been, shall we say

..."redecorated." There are fewer open spots from which to photograph them. There are also trees leaning on one another perilously close to falling. Bedrock is very close to the surface here and doesn't allow trees to deeply root. Therefore, they are easily toppled by wind or washed away during flash flooding.

The path begins at the southeast corner of the bridge and descends the roadside to creek level. At approximately 200' pass through a camping area with a fire ring. The pathway leaves the creek here for the steep hillside and parallels the creek's east (soon to be north) side at a distance that varies from 100 to 200'. The pathway has crude white blazes but is very hard to keep track of in places. At .15 of a mile cross a small wet-weather branch as you trace a hollow. At .35 of a mile cross another small branch while passing through a second hollow. At .45 of a mile arrive at the fall's viewing area.

3(a) Noontootla Falls

Roads: Graveled   A "4" 60' with cascades below
U.S.G.S. Quadrangle: Noontootla, Ga., no official trail, difficult

Directions: From the intersection of Doublehead Gap Road and Hwy. 60, take Doublehead Gap Road south approximately 5.7 miles to F.S. 58. Turn left and drive 3.1 miles to Noontootla Creek (the second creek past F.S. 58B). Keep a sharp eye out to the left for Noontootla's large boulders. Park here.

With hands free, make your way upstream 300' to observe the falls from a distance, as the cove gets much too steep for safety.

3(b) Long Creek Falls

Roads: Graveled   A "4" 20'
U.S.G.S. Quadrangle: Noontootla, Ga.
Appalachian Trail, 1 mile, 30 minutes, minor water crossings, moderate

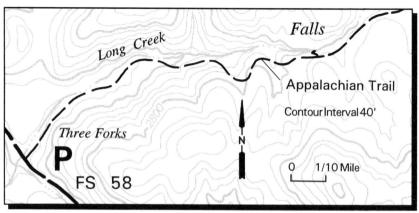

Directions: From Noontootla Creek, continue south on F.S. 58 for an additional 2.4 miles to the Appalachian Trail (Three Forks' parking area).

Hike northeast on the Appalachian Trail, which parallels Long Creek. The trail is level for the first 750´ then turns uphill and descends back to creek level. The trail now undulates and at the half-mile point crosses a wet-weather branch while outlining its hollow. At .7 of a mile cross another small branch. Next, the trail goes up and over a ridge line then descends to cross a third branch. In another .1 of a mile, after ascending steeply, look for the pathway to the falls on the left. Take this path for 300´ to the base of the falls.

This is a popular camping spot with a millstone serving as a fire ring.

Blue Ridge Area

Fall Branch Falls, Gilmer County, Georgia

Roads: Graveled   A "3" 50' two tiers
U.S.G.S. Quadrangle: Blue Ridge, Ga.
White blazed, .2 of a mile, 10 minutes, easy-moderate

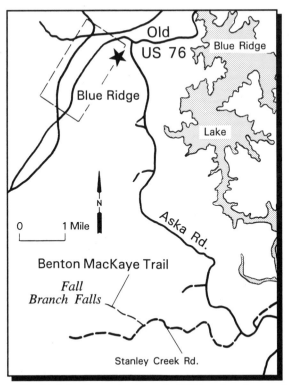

Note: Best seen shortly after rainfall.

Directions: From the intersection of Old U.S. 76 and Aska Road, approximately 1 mile east of downtown Blue Ridge, drive south on Aska Road for 8.2 miles to Stanley Creek Road (sign: "Rich Mountain Wildlife Management Area"). Turn right and drive 3.15 miles, passing the Warden's house, to a point where the Benton MacKaye Trail leaves the road to follow Fall Branch upstream (immediately after crossing the low bridge over Fall Branch). Park here.

Hike the Benton MacKaye Trail for just over .2 of a mile to a side trail which leads approximately 200´ to the observation deck at the base of the falls.

Land on the east side of the creek is privately owned.

Turners Corner Area

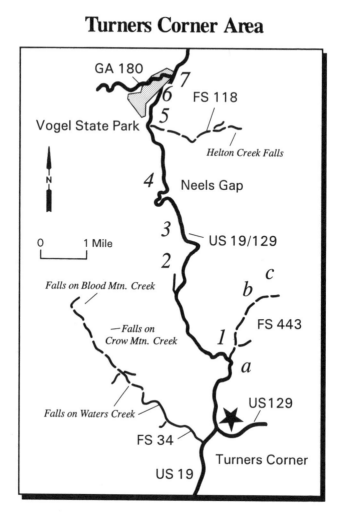

Falls on Waters Creek

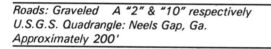

Roads: Graveled   A "2" & "10" respectively
U.S.G.S. Quadrangle: Neels Gap, Ga.
Approximately 200'

Directions: From Turners Corner (the intersection of U.S. Hwys. 19 and 129, 14.5 miles northeast of Dahlonega, and 10.6 miles northwest of Cleveland), take U.S. 19 south for .5 of a mile to Waters Creek Recreation Area (F.S. 34). Turn right and in 1.2 miles pass a roadside waterfall on the right. After viewing it, drive another 1.6 miles (2.8 miles total) to the second and more scenic waterfall. Park in the lot provided on the right.

Cross the road and hike the clearly-defined path down to the viewing area.

This is a super beauty with a large volume of water set against a backdrop of laurel and hemlock. Be careful on the sloping creekside bedrock as it is very slick.

For photographers, there is a spot .1 of a mile downstream where the falls are beautifully framed by overhanging trees and creek banks thick with rhododendron. To reach this spot, hike the road for .1 of mile and enter the woods on a slim path. The falls may be viewed from the rocks 150' away. A 70-135mm focal length would be handy here to compress the middle foreground rocks against the background waterfall and trees.

Falls on Crow Mountain Creek, Blood Mountain Wilderness

Roads: Graveled   A "3" 40' two tiers
U.S.G.S. Quadrangle: Neels Gap, Ga.
.8 of a mile, 20 minutes, water crossings, moderate

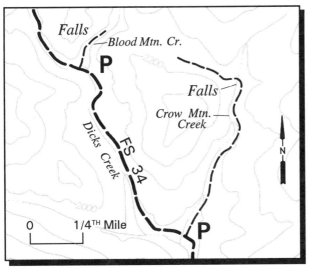

Directions: From the second waterfall on Waters Creek, continue up F.S. 34 for another .7 of a mile (a total of 3.5 miles from U.S. 19) to an old logging road on the right (approximately 200' before F.S. 34 fords Crow Mountain Creek). Park here. The route to the falls treads the logging road.

Although this is not a maintained hiking trail, it is wide and clear until the final approach to the falls. This last .1 of a mile has been blocked by windfalls. Recent storms have blown many trees down in north Georgia, making what were once easy hikes somewhat arduous, especially if you're carrying a backpack.

As you enter the woods cross a jeep-blocking mound. In just over .1 of mile cross a small year-round branch. After this crossing, the trail ascends steeply through a rocky cut and bends in lazy S fashion as it climbs the mountain. Slightly more than .2 of a mile into the hike the trail levels out then crosses another small branch. From here to the half-mile point the treadway ascends at an easy rate then bends slightly left. The rushing creek can be heard below. At .7 of a mile cross a wet-weather branch with a slim path up its right side. Here, the main trail bends sharply left and continues its ascent. The section just ahead was blocked by wind-fallen trees when I last visited. If the trail is still blocked, go uphill and around the exposed rootballs for easier walking. In another .1 of a mile make your way back down to the logging road. Listen carefully for the falls below then make your way through the woods to their base.

This long, shoaling waterfall is very pretty with adequate rainfall. Near the base I found a large but tricky rock to perch on, from which to photograph them.

Falls on Blood Mountain Creek, Blood Mountain Wilderness

Roads: Graveled/High Clearance   Lower A "5" 15', Upper A "6" 15'
U.S.G.S. Quadrangle: Neels Gap, Ga.
.1 of a mile, easy-moderate   See Falls on Crow Mtn. Creek for hiking map.

Directions: Follow the driving directions to the Falls on Crow Mountain Creek, but travel north an additional 1.1 miles on F.S. 34 (a total of 4.6 miles from U.S. 19). Cross Blood Mountain Creek on a culvert- and ford-like bridge and park. (There are flood gauges on this bridge. If water is up on these posts, don't attempt driving across! In flood the falls would be too dangerous for visitation anyway.)

Look for a slim path on the north side of the road leading up the left side of the creek. This path soon splits into several small paths. I found it best to stay uphill where the other paths turned down. Hike this steep pathway for 300'. As you arrive beside the lower falls descend to their base.

This portion of the waterfall is channeled through a narrow opening and splashes through a V in the rock, into an inverted V-shaped pool. The left side is flanked by small boulders and a steep bank. The right side features a 70' barren rock wall that rises out of the plunge pool at a 45° angle.

The upper falls are reached by hiking approximately 250' upstream, the last 70' of which is over scattered boulders. As you near the plunge pool, climb through a low spot in the boulders to access the fall's viewpoint.

The upper falls are more of a slide with a beautiful rock outcrop on the left. Where the rock is fissured, laurel and rhododendron have taken up residence.

There is a small but inaccessible waterfall seen from this vantage point further upstream.

Turners Corner - Vogel State Park Area

Directions: From Turners Corner (the intersection of U.S. Hwys. 19 and 129, 14.5 miles northeast of Dahlonega, and 10.6 miles northwest of Cleveland), take U.S. 19/129 north the following distances to access the points listed below. The following are located in Lumpkin County, Georgia, unless otherwise noted. See Area Map pg. 38.

1. F.S. 443, access to (a) the Falls on Buzzard Mountain Branch, (b) the Falls in the Little Ridge Area, and (c) the Falls in the Cowrock Creek Area: 1.45 miles.
2. The entrance to Desoto Falls Scenic Area: 4.15 miles.
3. The pullout on U.S. 19/129 with a view of Upper Desoto Falls: 5.8 miles.
4. The Walasi-Yi Center at Neels Gap: 7.9 miles.
5. Helton Creek Road (F.S. 118), access to Helton Creek Falls: 9.5 miles.
6. The entrance to Vogel State Park: 10.7 miles.
7. The intersection of Ga. Hwy. 180: 11.1 miles.

1(a) Falls on Buzzard Mountain Branch

Roads: Graveled   A "3" 25'
U.S.G.S. Quadrangle: Neels Gap, Ga.
.3 of a mile, water crossings, moderate-difficult

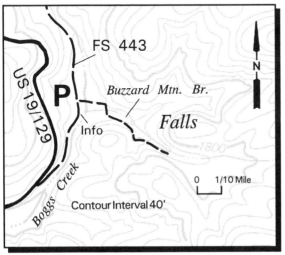

Directions: From U.S. 19/129 turn right onto F.S. 443 and drive for .3 of a mile, passing the information board, to the parking area on the left. There may be a dumpster at the north end of this parking area for further identification.

At this location look for a slim path on the right (east) side of 443 just upstream from the parking area. This leads to Boggs Creek and (if still in place) a large but slippery double log on which to cross the creek. If you need additional help in locating this dry crossing, walk back to the information board and pace off 255' (85 paces) then look for the worn pathway. (If the log is missing, walk back to the information board and wade the creek at the old vehicle ford located there. In this event, subtract 300' from the distances given below and pick up the hike at the asterisk* below.)

Upon crossing Boggs Creek, hike downstream. In 200' the path turns left to *follow Buzzard Mountain Branch upstream while paralleling the southern boundary of a wildlife opening for a short distance. The creek and path soon turn slightly right and head for deeper woods. At .2 of a mile, cross to the south side of the fall's branch on steppingstones and hike upstream via the remnants of an old logging road. In 200' the creek forks left and right at a point of land. This may go unnoticed as the creek on the left is obscured from view by the ever-thickening laurel. Take the right fork and round the hillside. From here on the thicket makes travel more difficult. The road plays out in the next hollow (.25 of a mile into the hike) and you're left to weave your way through the laurel and along the steep hillside for another 250' to the base of the falls.

This waterfall, like others in the area, has suffered storm damage, evidenced by wind-fallen trees. The cove is still very beautiful with beech, hemlock, and holly growing on its steep slopes. Plants to be found here include: ferns, galax, and Jack-in-the-pulpit. I especially liked the view from the base area looking downstream, where an overhanging, moss-covered rock outcrop has been undercut by the sharply bending creek. This is topped off by a lone towering hemlock whose roots are both splitting apart and holding the rock in place at the same time.

1(b) Falls in the Little Ridge Area

Roads: Graveled/High Clearance   A "6" collectively
U.S.G.S. Quadrangle: Neels Gap, Ga.
.6 of a mile, 20 minutes, water crossings, moderate

Directions: From the parking area for the Falls on Buzzard Mountain Branch, take F.S. 443 for 1.6 miles (or 1.9 miles total from U.S. 19/129) and park at the first ford. The pathway to the falls begins at a small camping area on the upstream (left) side of the road.

Cross the jeep-blocking mound and hike up what I call Little Ridge Creek on an old logging road. This road ascends moderately through a tunnel of rhododendron and crosses three branches, each of which are .1 of a mile apart. After crossing the third branch (just over .3 of a mile into the hike), pace off 300'. There, look carefully for a slim path leading 45° to the right. (The logging road veers noticeably left in this area of less dense woods. There may be a coffee table-size boulder in the road for further verification.) This leads approximately 100' to the creek bank then down to the best spot for crossing.

On the creek's east side, hike uphill to intersect a logging road which parallels Little Ridge Creek upstream. In .1 of a mile reach a point where the pathway steepens. The lower falls may be seen here. To view them close-up, make your

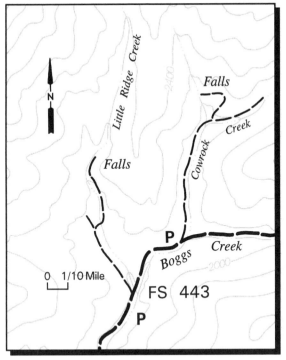

way through the woods down to their base. The middle and upper tiers lie 300 and 600' further up the logging road.

Atop the upper tier notice how the creek has worn the bedrock smooth, showing its beautiful grain. Also note the poplar tree that was blown over in its youth. This tree lies almost parallel to the ground but being a survivor shot its trunk towards the heavens in search of light. This is the sort of thing that intrigues me about nature. There is always something interesting and unusual to be found.

1(c) Falls in the Cowrock Creek Area

Roads: Graveled/High Clearance   A "2" 30'
U.S.G.S. Quadrangle: Neels Gap, Ga.   Shares Little Ridge hiking map.
.65 of a mile, 30 minutes, water crossings, easy

Directions: See directions to the Falls in the Little Ridge Area and continue north on F.S. 443 for an additional .35 of a mile to a sign "Road Closed." If the sign is missing, a ford will be straight ahead and an old logging road with jeep-blocking mounds will be to your left. Park here.

Cross the jeep-blocking mounds and hike the logging road following Cowrock Creek. The road serving as the trail ascends at an easy rate and in .5 of a mile crosses the western boundary of the Raven Cliffs Wilderness (denoted by white painted trees). Here also, the road crosses the fall's branch just above its confluence with Cowrock Creek. In approximately 100' take a slim path on the left (north) which crosses a small branch then leads alongside the fall's branch and towards a wildlife opening. Follow the tree line on the western edge of this opening for approximately 400' then reenter the woods on the far side. (You may notice the falls in the distance on the left.) Cross a small tributary of the fall's branch and veer left. Round the bottom of the hillside and in just over 200' arrive at the fall's viewing area.

2. Desoto Falls Scenic Area

Roads: Paved   U.S.G.S. Quadrangle: Neels Gap, Ga.
Lower A "4" moderate
Middle A "6" moderate
Upper A "4" moderate-difficult   See text for distances.

Directions: From U.S. 19/129 enter the Desoto Falls Scenic Area. The parking area and trailhead are on the immediate left. The trail begins at the information board at the north end of the lot.

Upon entering the woods the trail passes through a picnic area and makes a turn north. In 400' the trail shares the campground loop road, facing the one-way traffic. At 750' arrive at the footbridge over Frogtown Creek (the old trailhead).

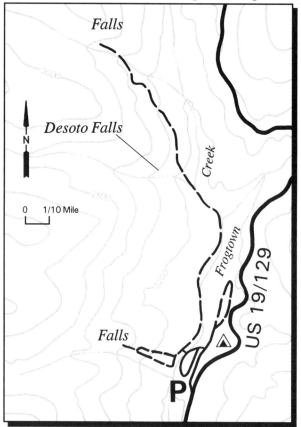

Cross to the west side of the creek. The trail to the middle and upper falls is on the right, while the lower fall's trail is on the left. Distances given below are from the footbridge.

Lower Falls Trail: From the footbridge, follow Frogtown Creek downstream. In just over 300' the return portion of the loop (which is discussed later) intersects on the right. At .1 of a mile the trail bends right to climb the fall's cove. At .15 of a mile arrive at steps and the apex of the loop. A side trail on the left leads 100' to the lower fall's observation deck.

The falls are small and pretty but recovering from the effects of recent storm damage. Not long ago this spot was covered with large trees.

Take the return trail which in 240' switchbacks down the mountainside. In another .1 of a mile arrive back at the entry portion of the loop. Backtrack to the footbridge for a total distance of .4 of a mile, including the side trail.

Middle Falls: For the most part the trail to the middle falls provides a pleasant undulating walk through a forest of hemlock and hardwoods while passing by several interesting rock outcrops.

From the footbridge, hike upstream. In just over .2 of a mile cross a footbridge over an unnamed branch. After hiking .7 of a mile arrive at a *second* footbridge. This crosses the middle fall's tributary. One-hundred feet from this bridge look for the side trail leading 200' up its cove to the observation deck.

Of the three falls in the scenic area, this is the most beautiful. Spilling in four tiers over granite ledges, the falls fade into the overhanging trees and mountainside.

Upper Falls: Return to the main trail and continue upstream. In just over .2 of a mile the trail narrows and turns noticeably uphill. The trail turns sharply left at .3 of a mile. In mid-summer, bluebell is found blooming on these higher, drier slopes. After hiking .6 of a mile from the middle falls (a total of 1.35 miles from the footbridge over Frogtown Creek) and gaining some 600' in elevation via steep grades and a pair of switchbacks, arrive at a point where the steeply-sliding falls are seen from the side.

Continue upstream for another .1 of a mile to a footbridge above the falls for a cool, well-deserved break.

3. Upper Desoto Falls Overlook

Look for the falls to the northwest across the valley.

4. Neels Gap (as above).

5. Helton Creek Falls, Union County, Georgia

Roads: Graveled   Lower A "3", Upper A "6"
U.S.G.S. Quadrangle: Coosa Bald, Ga.
850', minor water crossings, easy   No hiking map needed.

Directions: From U.S. 19/129 drive east on Helton Creek Road (F.S. 118). The pavement gives way to gravel in .75 of a mile. At 1.9 miles the road descends via hairpin turns. Continue for a total of 2.3 miles to the parking area on the right. The trail begins 100' west of the parking area.

Enter the woods on this descending trail and outline two hollows; the first at 300', the second at 500'. In another 100' arrive at the side trail leading to a bedrock viewing area of the 25', shoaling lower falls.

Return to the main trail, climb the steps, then cross a wet-weather branch while heading upstream. In 250' arrive at the base of the upper falls.

The upper falls shoal for 50' into a large and deep boulder-strewn pool.

They are especially beautiful after adequate rainfall. Catch the rhododendron on display here with a mid-summer visit.

6. Vogel State Park, Union County, Georgia
Trahlyta Lake Loop and Falls Bottom Trails

(Pronounced Trah-lee-tah)

Loop 1 mile, Falls Bottom Trail 650' one-way, easy-moderate
U.S.G.S. Quadrangle: Coosa Bald, Ga., Ga. fee area

Directions: From U.S. 19/129 turn left (west) into Vogel State Park. Parking for this loop trail is north of the entrance road, just across from the visitor center (near the helipad). The trail begins at the footbridge over Wolf Creek on the east side of the parking lot, near the #2 picnic area.

Upon crossing the footbridge the trail turns immediately left and closely follows the shoreline, at times treading boardwalks and steps. Right off, the lake's beautiful blue-green color catches the eye. Notice that even at the shoreline

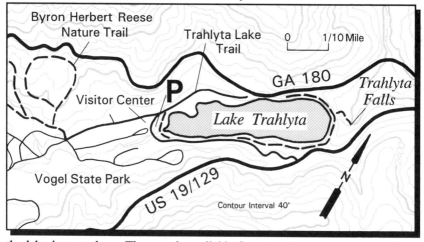

the lake is very deep. The woods available for a treadway are narrow at first, because of the lake's closeness to the entrance road. At .25 of a mile that changes as you enter a more scenic and wider stretch of woods. The forest is mixed, with stands of chestnut oak, dogwood, maple, white pine, and thickets of laurel. The girdling of some of the smaller trees along the lakeshore is evidence of beaver activity. In the early fall the trail is lined with blue clusters of bottle gentian. Thick patches of galax line it year-round. At .45 of a mile the trail exits the woods out onto the lake's earthen dam. After crossing the spillway on a wooden footbridge at the half-mile point, look for the Falls Bottom Trail approximately 100' ahead.

Hike this descending side trail for 650' to the Trahlyta Fall's observation deck.

This is a bright white, cascading, 40' waterfall set against dark granite. I saw white turtlehead in bloom for the first time, here.

Return to the Trahlyta Lake Trail and hike westerly to complete the loop. In .2 of a mile intersect the roadway near cabin #35. Hike the road for an additional .3 of a mile back to the parking area.

This waterfall may also be seen from U.S. 19/129 by driving north for .1 of a mile from the Vogel State Park entrance. Park on the west side of the highway at the southernmost pullout.

Byron Herbert Reese Nature Trail (Loop)

White blazed, .95 of a mile round trip visitor center and return, moderate

Note: Unless you are using Vogel's camping facilities please park at the visitor center and hike the campground access road to the trailhead. Directions given below are from the visitor center.

Hike the campground road for .2 of a mile to a point where the road splits. The trail enters the woods here via a stone stairway on the right (west) side of the road. This connecting trail is blazed flourescent green and winds while climbing at a moderate rate. After passing through a hollow the trail again climbs. At .3 of a mile arrive at a small woodland overlook perched 30' above a small creek. Just ahead lies the intersection of the Bear Hair, Coosa Backcountry, and the Byron Herbert Reese Nature Trail.

The white-blazed nature trail leads to the right. At .35 of a mile arrive at the point where the loop trail begins and ends. An aluminum plaque here tells of the local poet for whom the trail is named. Other plaques stationed along the trail make this an informative as well as scenic hike.

Hiking in a clockwise direction, the loop begins at a point of land and treads level like a contour line as it outlines a couple of hollows. At .45 of a mile pass red painted trees which denote the park's boundary. Nearing the half-mile point, the trail follows a small creek then treads a boardwalk before climbing steps up the north side of a hollow. The trail leads still further up and tops a ridge line. At .6 of a mile pass through an open stand of hickory, maple, oak and very large yellow poplar. Other trees seen here are hemlock, mountain magnolia, white pine, and small chestnut trees that early in life succumb to chestnut blight. Hopefully, we will again see this once dominant tree reclaim its rightful place in the forest.

At .65 of a mile a side trail leads left for 70' to benches atop a peaceful high point. At .7 of a mile cross a footbridge over a wet-weather branch. At .75 of a mile tie back into the beginning point of the loop.

7. Ga. Hwy. 180 (as above).

Helen - Hiawassee Area

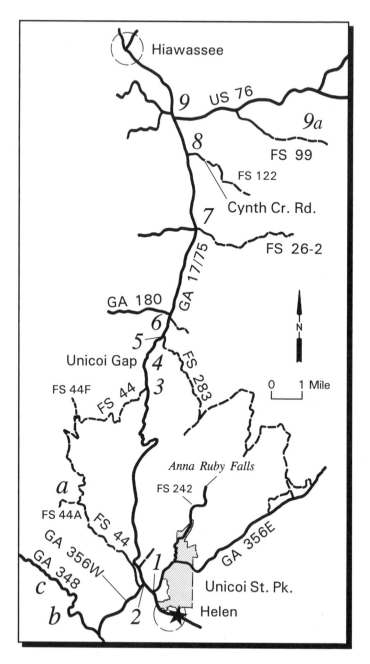

Hiawassee

9 US 76

9a

8 FS 99

FS 122

Cynth Cr. Rd.

7

FS 26-2

GA 180

GA 17/75

6

5

Unicoi Gap 4

FS 283

3

FS 44F

FS 44

N

0   1 Mile

Anna Ruby Falls

FS 242

a

FS 44A FS 44

GA 356E

GA 356W

GA 348

1

c

Unicoi St. Pk.

2

b

Helen

Directions: From the Chattahoochee River Bridge in downtown Helen, drive north on Ga. Hwy. 17/75 the following distances to these points of interest:

1. Ga. Hwy. 356 East, access to Anna Ruby Falls Scenic Area: 1.1 miles.
2. Ga. Hwy. 356 West (75 Alternate), access to (a) the Falls on Low Gap Creek, (b) Dukes Creek Falls, and (c) Raven Cliffs Falls: 1.5 miles.
3. F.S. 44, access to Horse Trough Falls: approximately 9.4 miles.
4. Unicoi Gap: 9.5 miles.
5. F.S. 283, access to High Shoals Falls Scenic Area: 11.5 miles.
6. Ga. Hwy. 180: 12.0 miles.
7. Mill Creek Road, access to Mill Creek Falls: 14.8 miles.
8. Cynth Creek Road, access to Fall Branch Falls: 17.2 miles.
9. U.S. 76 near Hiawassee: 18.4 miles. Take U.S. 76 east for 2.0 miles to:
    9(a) Swallow Creek Road, access to Fall Branch (Swallow Creek Area).

1. Anna Ruby Falls Scenic Area, White County, Georgia

Roads: Paved   A "10" U.S. fee area
U.S.G.S. Quadrangle: Tray Mountain, Ga.
Curtis Creek 153', York Creek 50'
.4 of a mile, moderate   No hiking map needed.

This is a special place to me as it is the first waterfall I ever saw. I visited this grand spot for the first time in 1966 while in Explorers. We camped atop the falls twice that year. Our leader, Mr. Mitchell, reverently told us how nature, starting with the mosses and lichens, worked to shape these mountains. ...mosses and lichens gained a toehold on the rock, he said, and by secreting acids they ate into solid rock allowing water an entry point. The freezing and thawing of water split the rock. In these cracks, he explained, humus became trapped and plants took root and further split the rock. These rocks were eventually broken down and ended up as the sands of the oceans to start the earth-building process anew. To this lowlander it was a fascinating story and I immediately fell in love with north Georgia's mountains. I was so impressed by the scenery that nine years later I brought my wife here on our honeymoon. I have been back many times since.

In those long-ago days there were not many visitors. There were, however, pathways leading to the cliff tops of both York and Curtis Creeks. For safety reasons those paths have been blocked off and have long since been reclaimed by the forest. I admit they were very dangerous. One misstep while hopping the slick rock atop York Creek and it would've been over the falls we go.

Anna Ruby Falls is named for the only daughter of a Confederate Colonel, John H. (Captain) Nichols. Captain Nichols owned these lands. His Victorian-era residence still stands just east of the intersection of Ga. Hwys. 17 and 75 at Nacoochee.

The area was logged in the early part of this century. Draft animals and steam-powered winches called "Steam Donkeys" pulled logs over the rough terrain to railheads to be transported out. One such logging rail line ran alongside Smith Creek to the base of the falls. Many creeks in our southern mountains had these rail lines up their coves. Being a railroad man myself, I'll bet trees and man alike lost limbs up these hollows. The journey out of these hills had to be hair-raising on those ragged, make-shift rail lines.

Back in the late 1970's an interesting local man told me that during the gold rush days of the 1840's, water from the falls was diverted via a series of flumes for nearby hydraulic gold mining.

Directions: From Hwy. 17/75 take Hwy. 356 East for 1.35 miles to F.S. 242, on the left. A sign located here announces "Anna Ruby Falls Scenic Area." Drive 242 for 3.5 miles to its end and park at the visitor center. The paved trail begins at the north end of the parking area.

This is a leisurely hike with trailside plaques describing plants, trees, and past logging activities in the area. The trail follows the beautiful, rushing Smith Creek upstream. After hiking .1 of a mile, cross a footbridge to the east side of the creek. The trail steepens, then at the quarter-mile point levels out as it rounds an outcrop of huge boulders. Hemlocks rooted in the cracked rock enhance their beauty. The trail then undulates and at .4 of a mile arrives at the observation decks. (The blue-blazed Smith Creek Trail intersects here as well. This trail leads 5.0 miles to Unicoi State Park.)

This is one of the most visited and photographed waterfalls in Georgia. I've even seen the falls on the pages of an out-of-state travel brochure where they were claimed (probably without their knowledge) as being from that locale.

The best luck I've had photographing this setting was in the afternoon on a cold, clear winter's day. Those conditions afforded me plenty of blue sky and white water. A wide-angle lens is needed to capture this double waterfall in a single frame. A perspective control lens is needed to avoid keystoning.

2(a) Falls on Low Gap Creek, Mark Trail Wilderness, White County, Georgia

---
Roads: High Clearance   A "5"
U.S.G.S. Quadrangle: Jacks Gap, Ga.
No official trail, .75 of a mile, water crossings, moderate

Note: Low Gap Creek (where crossed by F.S. 44A) may be too deep to ford in a vehicle after heavy rains. (See below*.)

Return towards Helen unless you plan to see Horse Trough Falls, the turnoff for which is 5.5 miles ahead. F.S. 44 doesn't tie back in to pavement for more than 10 miles.

Be especially careful hiking along Low Gap Creek as there are exposures with 10' drops.

Directions: From Ga. Hwy. 17/75 take Hwy. 356 West and immediately cross the Chattahoochee River Bridge. In .1 of a mile turn right onto Chattahoochee River Road (F.S. 44). Drive north for 4.4 miles to F.S. 44A. *Turn left and in .2 of a mile ford Low Gap Creek. Continue for a total of .65 of a mile to the camping area and gate at the second ford. Park in the lot provided so as to not block the gate. The pathway to the falls begins at the gate and ford.

Cross Low Gap Creek on foot via the concrete ford. In 250' the roadbed bends sharply left while the pathway to the falls (an old jeep road) enters the woods and

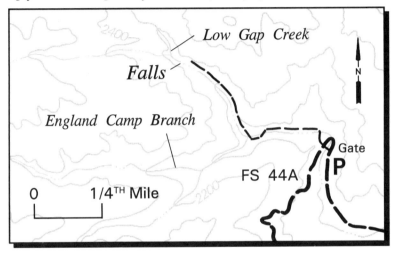

parallels the south side of the creek. At 440' cross to the north side of Low Gap Creek. Once across, hike upstream immediately crossing a wet-weather branch. (From this point to the next ford [.2 of a mile away] the pathway is in and out of bogs and if there has been recent rainfall may be in the creek's overflow.) One-quarter mile into the hike, again cross the creek, this time to the south side. Hike upstream and make the last ford at .35 of a mile, just below the confluence of England Camp and Low Gap Creeks.

Narrowing to a single track, the pathway becomes much more rugged as it follows Low Gap Creek upstream. At .4 of a mile the path drops to creek level where hiking becomes a lesson in the art of ducking, bobbing, and weaving through the laurel. Nearing the half-mile point notice a 6' shoaling cascade. There are more just ahead. The pathway heads uphill to parallel the creek at a distance of 50 to 60' and some 30' above creek level. At .6 of a mile cross a small wet-weather branch, then another one 250' further. After crossing the second branch, the path tops a small rise. The mountainsides are now getting steeper. At .7 of a mile note an unusual (for this locale) flat spot. The lower falls are approximately 100' ahead. To reach their base, carefully descend the hillside and bypass the slick and sloping boulders en route to creek level.

The splash pool's bedrock is rich in browns, while the cliffs and boulders are adorned with emerald-green mosses.

The upper tier is reached by hiking upstream for 200'. En route, cross the base of a couple of small ridges that are slippery with loose rock and topsoil. Between these ridges the pathway ventures down to the creek's bedrock.

The upper falls are a 60'-long waterslide with a total drop of 20'. There is a large and beautiful lichen-covered boulder on the right side which overhangs their base.

To photograph the lower falls, avoid the contrast of the mountains' shadows with an early morning or late afternoon, late summer visit. (The diffused lighting of an overcast day also works well.) Lesser amounts of water at that time of year don't overwhelm the beautiful rock. Also, the surrounding forest is still green and filled out, providing a backdrop that would otherwise be rendered on film as washed-out skies.

2(b) Dukes Creek Falls, White County, Georgia

Roads: Paved   A "7" 200'+
U.S.G.S. Quadrangle: Cowrock, Ga.
1.2 miles, moderate

Directions: From Ga. Hwy. 17/75 drive west on Hwy. 356 for 2.35 miles to the Richard Russell Scenic Hwy. (Ga. 348). Turn right and drive 1.7 miles to the Dukes Creek Fall's parking area (a sign marks the entrance) on the left. In .15 of a mile arrive at the trailhead at the apex of this loop road.

New trail construction and a major face lift have made this already beautiful spot a real showpiece. The unsightly shortcuts and crisscrossing informal paths that were eroding the hillsides have been eliminated by the trail's new route. Viewing the falls has been made better, safer, and easier as well.

As you leave the parking area, the paved trail descends two flights of steps and turns right. Paralleling the entrance road, in .1 of a mile arrive at the upper observation deck. Dukes Creek Falls (actually located on Davis Creek) may be seen across the valley approximately 800' away. This is the least obstructed view of the upper portion of the falls. (As the trail descends trees block them from view.)

At .15 of a mile the trail leaves the boardwalk and descends still further while treading an old graveled roadbed. Now following alongside Hwy. 348, at .35 of a mile arrive at a flight of steps. At their base the trail turns sharply left to follow Dodd Creek downstream. (I found a sign here stating "Falls" with an arrow pointing left.) The trail runs fairly level to the half-mile point while the creek itself drops. At .6 of a mile pass by a cascade which is heard below on Dodd Creek. At .65 of a mile Dukes Creek Falls can be seen through the trees across the gorge.

The trail bends left and rounds the mountainside, then at .85 of a mile makes a hard right and leaves the roadbed. Narrowing to a single track, the trail now descends at a more moderate rate. The forest changes from hardwoods, found on higher ground, to more moisture tolerant Fraser magnolia, hemlock, and white pine. After a brief absence the sound of rushing water returns. At 1.1 miles the trail undulates while passing under a canopy of laurel and rhododendron. Just ahead lies one of the grandest structures that I've ever set foot on—a beautifully designed boardwalk leading to the observation decks for both Dukes (on the left) and Dodd Creek Falls (straight ahead). If visiting in winter be careful on this potentially icy deck.

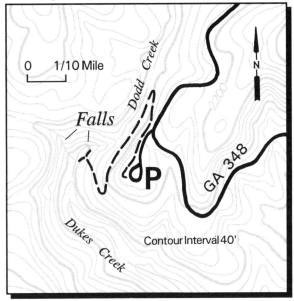

The falls on Dodd Creek are approximately 15' high and 10' wide with a very pretty, steep exposure of bedrock and high mountainsides as a backdrop. After splashing into a small pool, the creek slides over polished granite then cascades into the green-tinted waters of stone-filled pools below.

Dukes Creek Falls are seen from the lower deck through a veil of hemlock and rhododendron. This beautiful waterfall is split into multiple cascading flows. At their base the waters of Davis and Dodd Creeks commingle to form Dukes Creek, their juncture marked by an overhanging boulder embraced in roots of hemlock.

2(c) Raven Cliffs Falls, Raven Cliffs Wilderness, White County, Georgia

Roads: Paved   A "10" collectively
U.S.G.S. Quadrangle: Cowrock, Ga.
Trail #22, blue blazed, 2.55 miles, minor water crossings, moderate

Directions: See Dukes Creek Falls and add the directions given below to them.

From the Dukes Creek Fall's parking area, drive west on Ga. Hwy. 348 for 1.25 miles to an unmarked grassy parking area on the left. (The highway's 3 milepost [if intact] will be directly across the roadway at this location.) Park here. The trail enters the woods over jeep-blocking mounds on the Bear Den Creek side of the parking area.

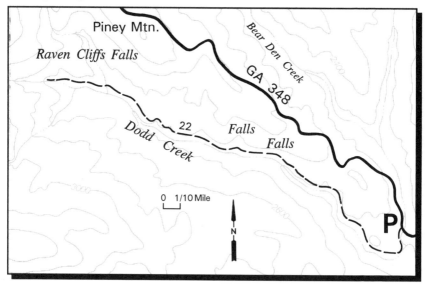

Upon entering the woods the Raven Cliffs Trail descends then levels while paralleling Bear Den Creek. There may be a wooden sign here announcing "Raven Cliffs Wilderness." At 425' cross a small branch and veer right as the trail enters the Dodd Creek drainage. (There are several confusing paths here because of heavy use by campers.) The trail now parallels the north side of a sometimes placid, often noisy and rushing Dodd Creek, upstream to the falls.

At .3 of a mile pass the first large rock outcrop (20' in length and 10' high). Dodd Creek flows by on the left in a series of beautiful cascades with a total drop of 10'. In spots where the creek flows fast and clear over bedrock, swirling veins of quartz are seen in its dark, water-polished granite.

What you can expect from this point on, is a sometimes tough trail that undulates up and down, then left and right, while passing through open woods and narrow tunnels of rhododendron sporting slick roots, not to mention the half-dozen logs that must be straddled, to which hatchet-bearing campers have taken a passing whack. You'll also encounter numerous small creek crossings and springs that percolate to the surface, as well as several overused primitive campsites. Aside from these minor drawbacks, the scenery along the way and at the trail's end is among the most beautiful in Georgia.

Commonly found here are American holly, hemlock, maple, poplar, and the flower cinquefoil. Rare finds include American basswood, trillium, and trout lily.

Continuing upstream, pass alternating placid and rushing stretches of creek then at 1.1 miles arrive at the lower falls.

This waterfall spills over a 15' rock face in an open bedrock area. A pathway leads down to creek level for an unobstructed view.

Again continuing upstream, the second falls lie just .2 of a mile ahead. En route to them, the trail ascends to a point high above the creek. This 30' waterfall comes into view and is best seen as it is approached on the main trail. There is a pathway down the cliff to the base, but it is steep and dangerous.

Hiking upstream, the main trail is again in and out of a canopy of rhododendron and in the next half mile crosses several small branches and creeks that flow off of Piney Mountain.

At 1.9 miles pass several primitive camping areas. Cross a large year-round creek at 2.15 miles. In just over .1 of a mile the trail turns noticeably uphill. Topping out in 300' the trail descends and levels on a fern-covered hillside. After crossing a small branch, the trail bends sharply right entering a hollow, then left to climb the steep fall's cove. Look for a slim path at 2.45 miles leading to a creekside view of the cascades below the cliffs. This three-tier cascade is seen up close from the main trail in 200'.

While investigating the cascade, notice that the massive cliffs lean 5° to the north and have joint-type fissures that run from top to bottom. Their east face is covered heavily in toadskin lichen. The base is littered with huge chunks of the former cliffs.

The trail continues its climb and terminates at the fall's viewing area.

The 30' upper falls spill into the dark, mystical, mossy split of two huge blocks of granite and careen into a small plunge pool. It appears to me that in the past these two blocks were one, with the creek flowing over it. Over the eons freezing and thawing split their faults, and the east block fell then slumped away from the larger mass.

The best conditions to photograph this waterfall are after considerable rainfall. In the dry months it's barely a trickle. An overcast day is needed for even lighting. On bright days the cliffs overexpose, even though they face north, while the waterfall underexposes in deep shadows.

This scenic area needs our help. Thoughtless campers, hikers, and rappellers are taking a tragic toll here. Please stay on existing trails. If camping, bring a stove. Please!, no climbing or rappelling—the delicate mosses and lichens adorning the cliffs can't tolerate the traffic.

3. Horse Trough Falls, Mark Trail Wilderness, Union County, Georgia

Roads: Graveled   A "6" 70'
U.S.G.S. Quadrangle: Jacks Gap, Ga.
Blue blazed, 800', easy

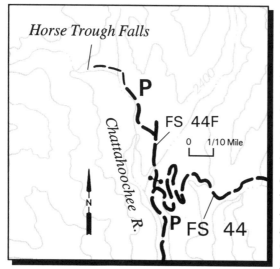

Horse Trough Falls

Directions: From Ga. Hwy. 17/75 turn left (west) onto F.S. 44 and check your mileage. In .3 of a mile, on the right, notice a small cascading wet-weather waterfall on Spoilcane Creek. At 3.4 miles pass a very nice waterfall to the left on Wilks Creek. Drive a total of 4.75 miles to F.S. 44F, which is on the right. Take 44F (which in 150' crosses a bridge over Henson Creek) through the campground to the fall's parking area .4 of a mile ahead. The trail to the falls begins at the apex (north end) of the loop road. (If the campground access road [F.S. 44F] is gated, park in the pullout on the right just before the gate and hike the road with the above directions.)

Enter the woods and in 150' cross the Chattahoochee River on a footbridge. Soon thereafter, the trail enters the cove of Little Horse Trough Creek, paralleling the creek's north side. Just ahead, in winter, while peering over winterberry, the distant falls come into view. After hiking a total of 600' arrive at the lower cascades and descend the rock ledge to creek level. Carefully work your way up the right side of the creek on slick bedrock to the base of the falls 200' away.

The falls flow full bore after winter rains and churn up a mist-laden breeze that rustles the surrounding rhododendron, making long exposures difficult. In summer, the cove is deeply shaded with high-contrast shafts of light penetrating the darkness. Additionally, tree limbs and vegetation block some of the view.

4. Unicoi Gap (as above).

5. High Shoals Falls Scenic Area, Towns County, Georgia

Roads: Graveled   An "8" & "4" respectively
U.S.G.S. Quadrangle: Tray Mountain, Ga.
Blue blazed, 1.2 miles, moderate-difficult

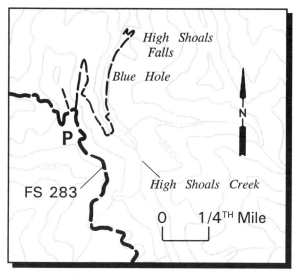

Directions: From Ga. Hwy. 17/75 make a hard right turn (east) onto F.S. 283 and in .15 of a mile ford the Hiawassee River. Drive up the mountainside for a total of 1.3 miles to the parking area and trailhead, which is on the left. There may be a sign here announcing "High Shoals Falls 1 mile." (If the sign is missing, look for two in-ground trash cans. There is also a pathway leading straight ahead to a high point on the ridge.) The trail to the falls begins on the right (east) side of this ridge.

After descending at a moderate rate for just over .2 of a mile, the trail turns sharply right and enters a deep and very scenic hollow of hardwoods and hemlock. At .35 of a mile cross a dripping spring-like branch in the hollow's depths. The trail then outlines a lesser hollow and descends at a moderate rate. Slightly more than .5 of a mile into the hike the treadway turns sharply left as it nears a small branch. Just ahead, the trail again bends sharply left to now follow High Shoals Creek downstream, albeit at a distance. At .6 of a mile the trail crosses the creek on a footbridge and treads its east side on an old roadbed. Fire rings among the open stand of white pines attest to the popularity of this spot for camping. At .7 of a mile cross a small trickling branch on a footbridge, then just ahead pass over a plank-type walkway. This stretch of the trail is lined with galax and passes under a canopy of hemlock and laurel. The trail which has been fairly level from the first footbridge, now at .9 of a mile, begins a steep descent. As you approach Blue Hole Falls, the treadway makes a slight right turn and descends to cross a small branch on a footbridge. Just shy of a mile, notice a large boulder in the middle of the trail and a rock outcrop on the right. In 100', look for the side trail which leads 150' to the observation deck and base of Blue Hole Falls.

Return to the main trail and continue downstream. In less than a tenth of a mile the trail bends sharply left (the old roadbed continues straight ahead leading to private property). Descend via a series of switchbacks to the High Shoals Fall's observation deck and the trail's end .2 of a mile away.

57

From high up the mountainside, High Shoals Creek shoots out of the laurel and hemlocks as a 50'-long cascade that steepens into a 40' fall down the rock face. The bulk of its flow is over the left side with two smaller rivulets on the right. In the dry months the falls are channeled entirely over the left side through a solitary flume.

Both falls are very beautiful when seen under the right conditions. I like Blue Hole best when the creek is down to a moderate level and not overwhelming the surrounding scenery. High Shoals, on the other hand, is at its best just after heavy rainfall.

6. Georgia Hwy. 180 (as above).

7. Mill Creek Falls, Towns County, Georgia

Roads: Graveled/High Clearance   A "6"
U.S.G.S. Quadrangle: Tray Mountain, Ga.
No official trail, 800', moderate (steep grade, short distance)

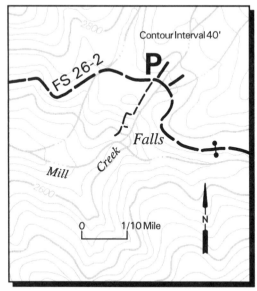

Directions: From Ga. Hwy. 17/75 turn right (east) onto Mill Creek Road and drive 1.1 miles to F.S. 26-2. Turn left. Reset your odometer and after traveling .65 of a mile enter the Swallow Creek Wildlife Management Area. If the road is gated, it will be here. Two and one-half miles from the pavement the road crosses Mill Creek. Look for a camping area on the right and the pullouts on the left and right sides of the road. Park here. (F.S. 26-2 ends at a gate in another .2 of a mile.)

Hike through the primitive camping area approximately 70' away. The path is hard to detect but generally follows the west side of Mill Creek downstream at a distance of 50 to 60'. In 450' the path exits the woods near the top of the falls. To circumvent the cliff face, turn right. In 50' the pathway turns left and descends very steeply through the laurel thicket. This path has offshoots leading

58

to the base of both the upper and lower falls which are 150 and 300' away respectively.

This location is best seen after being charged up by heavy rainfall. Under this condition the rock faces are filled from one side to the other with sliding surges of white water. The best time to see and photograph them is on a clear winter's day from noon to 2:00 PM. This is when the best frontal lighting occurs. At other times of day heavy shadows are present.

Over the centuries Mill Creek's abrasiveness has polished the granite face, exposing its beautiful wood-like grain and randomly crisscrossing white bands of quartzite.

8. Fall Branch Falls, Towns County, Georgia

Roads: Graveled/High Clearance   A "2"
U.S.G.S. Quadrangle: Macedonia, Ga.
Seen from car.

Note: F.S. 122 lacks a turnaround.

Directions: From Ga. Hwy. 17/75 turn right (east) onto Cynth Creek Road (200' south of the Hiawassee River Bridge) and drive .5 of a mile to a point where the road forks. Veer right. In another 1.15 miles turn left onto the lightly graveled F.S. 122. This road can be driven, if careful, in a car with adequate clearance. (Don't let the clear-cut, burned-off hillsides first encountered scare you off. The fall's cove is intact.) Follow 122 for .75 of a mile to the falls which are on the left.

The falls slide and cascade in a cove of large, lichen-covered boulders. The setting is at its best when the leaves are off— a blue-sky winter's day after heavy rainfall is just right. Summer's growth hides much of the beauty found here.

When photographing, wait for the afternoon sun to provide even lighting. Keystoning is a major problem here.

The next problem is getting turned around. I had to wiggle my truck back and forth across the roadway to get headed back out.

9. U.S. 76 (as above).

9(a) Fall Branch (Swallow Creek Area), Towns County, Georgia

Roads: Graveled/High Clearance   A "5"
U.S.G.S. Quadrangle: Macedonia, Ga.
No official trail, .2 of a mile, water crossing, moderate

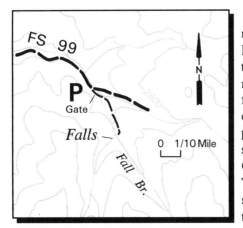

Directions: At this location turn right (south) onto Swallow Creek Road (sign: "Lower Hightower Baptist Church"). After driving 1.85 miles arrive at a point where the road forks and the pavement ends. (I consider the right half of the fork a private driveway.) There may be a sign here announcing "Swallow Creek Wildlife Management Area." Take the left fork (F.S. 99) and soon ford Swallow Creek. Enter the Chattahoochee National Forest as you pass through the gate. At 2.9 miles a road intersects from the right. Stay left. Drive a total of 3.65 miles from U.S. 76 (fording the creek three more times en route) to the parking area on the right. Look for a gate 50' south of the parking area where the pathway to the falls (an old logging road) begins.

Standing at the gate, notice that this old roadbed crosses Fall Branch diagonally and enters an obscure tunnel-like opening in the laurel just upstream. After crossing, hike the ascending path upstream for 250' where another logging road will intersect from the left. Stay to the right and continue upstream for an additional 750' and listen for the falls on the right. (Foliage may obscure them from view during the summer months.) A path then leads down to a viewpoint 150' away.

This deeply-shaded location photographs best on an overcast day, or in the late afternoon when the sun's piercing light can no longer reach the cove's depths. I like this hidden waterfall best in the summer when everything is greened up— it reminds me of the tropics.

Clayton West

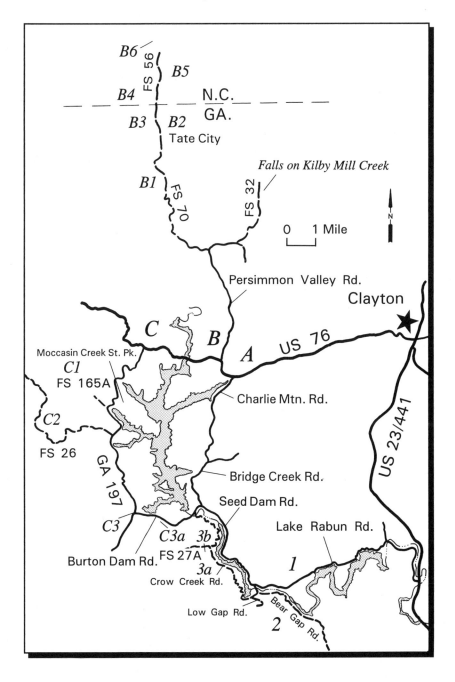

This section is broken into three routes with distances from U.S. 441 in Clayton. Take U.S. 76 West to these access points.

Unless otherwise noted, the falls listed below are located in Rabun County, Georgia.

   A. Charlie Mountain Road (access to the waterfalls in the Lake Rabun and Seed Lake areas): 7.3 miles.

   B. Persimmon Valley Road, a.k.a. Persimmon Road (the waterfalls in the Southern Nantahala Wilderness area, Georgia access); (access to the Falls on Kilby Mill Creek): 8.2 miles. Text for "B" begins on pg. 65.

   C. Ga. Hwy. 197 (access to the Falls on Moccasin Creek, Wildcat Creek, and Horse Branch): 11.4 miles. Text for "C" begins on pg. 72.

A. Directions: Turn left onto Charlie Mountain Road from U.S. 76 and proceed 3.6 miles to Bridge Creek Road. Turn right and drive 1.9 miles to Seed Dam Road*. (The Georgia Power Land Office is located at this intersection.) Turn left onto Seed Dam Road (which soon changes to Lake Rabun Road), this time traveling 6.15 miles to the Rabun Beach Campground's area #2 entrance, which is on the left.

The Rabun Beach Campground is the beginning point for the waterfalls listed below.

   1. Panther and Angel Falls (see directions below).

   2. Minnehaha Falls (see directions below).

   3(a) Falls on Bad Branch (see directions below).

   3(b) Crow Creek Falls (see directions below).

1. Panther and Angel Falls

Roads: Paved   A "7" & "9" respectively
U.S.G.S. Quadrangle: Tiger, Ga., minor water crossings
Trail #55, Panther Falls .6 of a mile, easy-moderate
Angel Falls additional .3 of a mile, moderate-difficult

Note: Best seen after rainfall. Campground gated in winter.

Directions: Enter the Rabun Beach Campground's area #2 entrance and hike (if gated for the winter) or drive the one-way loop road for approximately .2 of a mile to a grassy parking area on the right, at the road's apex. There may be a sign here "Trail Parking." The trailhead (visible from the parking area) is 80' to the north.

As you enter the woods cross a footbridge to the west side of Joe Creek. While here, notice the stairstep-type cascade that runs for 80' while dropping approximately 15'. Use this as a waterfall barometer. If this cascade is white and

*See item "C3(a)" (Falls on Horse Branch) pg. 72.

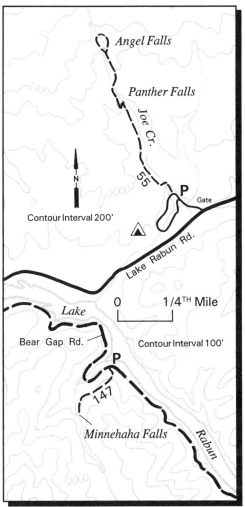

beautiful with water, Panther and Angel Falls will be spectacular. If Joe Creek is not flowing heavily, this cascade may be just an unexciting trickle flowing over small rock ledges.

The trail climbs steeply alongside this cascade, tops out then drops back to creek level. While passing through an open area the trail narrows through a stretch of knee- to waist-high vegetation. At .2 of a mile you can again see your feet as you pass beneath a canopy of laurel. The creek makes several slides in this area. At .3 of a mile cross a small wet-weather branch via a boardwalk. After crossing a couple of small tributaries the trail begins an easy ascent. At .5 of a mile cross to the east side of Joe Creek on a footbridge. The trail now starts up at a more moderate rate. In another 200' cross a footbridge back to the west bank. After hiking a total of .6 of a mile arrive at Panther Falls.

The falls tumble from right to left over dozens of ledges before landing in a shallow, sandy pool. They are easily seen from a bedrock exposure just downstream from their base.

To reach Angel Falls, return to the main trail which immediately climbs a steep switchback alongside Panther Falls. Now atop the falls and paralleling the creek, the trail soon passes through open woods. At .8 of a mile cross a small tributary then just ahead the larger Joe Creek. In approximately 250' arrive at the downstream point of the loop. Either route, right or left, leads steeply to the observation deck 150' away.

Seen with adequate water, this is one of the finest sights in the book.

The falls photograph best under the diffused lighting of an overcast day or in the shadows of early morning or late afternoon. If the sun is high overhead there is too much contrast.

2. Minnehaha Falls, Falls Branch Trail

Roads: Graveled   An "8"   See Panther and Angel Falls pg. 63 for hiking map.
U.S.G.S. Quadrangle: Tiger-Tallulah Falls, Ga. in their margins
Trail #147, .2 of a mile, easy-moderate

Directions: See directions to the Rabun Beach Campground and proceed from there.

Take Lake Rabun Road west (backtracking) for 1.7 miles. Turn left onto Low Gap Road (the first road downstream from the Seed Lake Dam). Drive .15 of a mile, crossing a one-lane bridge en route to a three-way intersection (stop signs)*. Take the graveled road straight ahead (Bear Gap Road). This generally follows Lake Rabun's shoreline. After driving 1.5 miles look for the pullout on the left (as you are exiting a sharp curve to the left) and the trail's in-ground steps on the right. The trailhead may be marked by a carsonite stake.

The trail enters the woods via the steps then climbs at a moderate rate. Topping out in approximately .1 of a mile, the trail descends slightly, bends left then ascends again. After hiking a total of .2 of a mile arrive at the base of the falls.

Minnehaha is considered by many to be Rabun County's prettiest. It falls in stair-step fashion, like others in the area, but with a much larger volume of water.

*See Falls on Bad Branch and Crow Creek Falls (below).

3(a) Falls on Bad Branch

Roads: Graveled   A "9"   25'
U.S.G.S. Quadrangle: Lake Burton, Ga.   No hiking map needed.
No official trail, 900', 10 minutes, easy

Directions: Return to the three-way intersection (stop signs)* described in Minnehaha. Turn left. This is Low Gap Road. Take this road for just over .3 of a mile and turn right onto Crow Creek Road where a sign reads "Georgia Power Recreation Area 4 miles." Follow this road for 2.95 miles to a pullout on the right. (There is a small road on the left at 2.9 miles that looks similar to and could be confused with the roadbed serving as the pathway to Bad Branch. Be sure to drive the full 2.95 miles.) For further help in finding the correct pullout, look for a power pole on the right with the I.D. numbers 41-50. The pathway to the falls (an old roadbed, seen from the road as you round a left bend) is level and intersects the road from the left at a 45° angle.

Hike the level path and in 700' pass by an old concrete foundation (the remnants of a C.C.C. camp). In another 100' pass a popular camping spot on the right. The pathway narrows while leading an additional 100' to the base of the falls.

Although the falls are not large; they are a giant in the beauty department, with lots of moss, weeping rocks, and a wall on the left draped in the greenery of aquatic plants.

Virgin Falls, Tennessee
Nikon FM2, Nikkor 24-50 @ 24mm, *f*/16, Kodak T-Max 100 @ 1/2 sec.

Little River Falls, Ala., Nikon FM2, Nikkor 24-50 Zoom @ 30mm, *f*/11, Fuji RDP 100 rated @ ISO 200, exposed @ 1/60TH sec. Taken after a good rain.

Blue Hole Falls, Grundy State Forest, Tn., Nikon FG, Fuji Velvia (ISO 50), exposure unrecorded.

Anna Ruby Falls, Georgia

Desoto Falls, Alabama

Lost Falls, Desoto State Park, Ala.
Nikon FG, Nikkor 24-50 Zoom @ 24mm,
f/22, Fuji Velvia (ISO 50), @ 1 sec. Taken
after a good rain.

W/F #1, Cloudland Canyon St. Pk., Ga.
Nikon FG, Nikkor 24-50 Zoom @ 30mm,
f/22, Fuji RDP 100, @ 1 sec.

The cliffs at Raven Cliffs Falls, Nikon
FG, Nikon 50mm lens, f/16, Fuji Velvia (ISO
50) @ 1/15TH sec., polarizer.

Falls on Emery Creek, Nikon FM2,
Nikkor 20mm, f/16, Fuji RDP 100, @ 1 sec.

Falls on Low Gap Creek

Falls on Bad Branch

Sulfurous Polyporous on Woodland Log,
Fuji Velvia (ISO 50), Nikkor 24-50 Zoom @
24mm, exposure unrecorded.

Panther Falls, Ga.
Fuji RFP 50, exposure unrecorded.

Amicalola Falls State Park, Ga., Nikon
FM2, Nikkor 24-50 Zoom, Fuji RDP 100.

**Piney Creek Falls, Fall Creek Falls St.
Pk., Tn.,** Nikon FM2, Sigma 28-135 zoomed
to 60mm, $f/11$, Fuji RDP 100, @ 1/2 sec.

Blue Hole, High Shoals Falls S. A.

Denton Creek Falls

Ozone Falls, Tennessee
Nikon FG, Nikkor 24-50, @ 24mm, *f*/16, Kodak T-Max 100 @ 1 sec.

3(b) Crow Creek Falls

Roads: Graveled   A "5" 10'
U.S.G.S. Quadrangle: Lake Burton, Ga.   No hiking map needed.
No official trail, 350', easy

Directions: From the Falls on Bad Branch, take Crow Creek Road an additional .95 of a mile to F.S. 27A on the left. (I found a carsonite stake marking the road. For further verification a power pole on the lake side of the road has the I.D. numbers 41-72 on it.) Travel .2 of a mile on 27A and park. Look for an old roadbed on the left (south) that enters the woods and leads downhill. This serves as the pathway to the falls.

Enter the woods and in approximately 30' the old roadbed forks left and right. Take the left fork and hike downstream for 245'. Look for a slim pathway, on the right, leading 75' to the base of the falls.

This waterfall spills over four small ledges and flows into a shallow, sandy-bottomed pool surrounded by dense rhododendron. Its moss-covered rock face is approximately 40' wide. A steep mountain slope with hemlock trees and chestnut stumps flanks the left side.

B. Directions: From U.S. 76, turn right onto Persimmon Valley Road (the Tallulah - Persimmon Volunteer Fire Department is located at this intersection) and drive 4.2 miles to F.S. 70 which is on the left. A sign here announces "Southern Nantahala Wilderness 9 miles."

Listed below are the points of interest and their respective distances from Persimmon Valley Road via F.S. 70. (F.S. 70 changes to F.S. 56 at the North Carolina state line.) The road surface is graveled.

B1. The Tate Branch Campground: 4.1 miles.
B2. Access to Denton Creek Falls: 6.55 miles.
B3. Access to Fall Branch Falls (primitive campground): 6.7 miles.
B4. The North Carolina state line: 7.4 miles.
B5. Parking and trailhead for Trail #378 to Bull Cove, Bear Creek, and High Falls: 7.8 miles.
B6. Boulders blocking the road and trailhead for Trail #377 (access to Thomas Falls): 9.0 miles.

Use the Tate Branch Campground, or the mileage at the N.C. state line as reference points.

Note: In the area around Tate City, please be courteous to the locals and park only where signs permit. Otherwise you may end up with your car being towed as my friend Bob did.

B1. Tate Branch Campground (as above).

B2. Denton Creek Falls,
Towns County, Georgia

Map: Southern Nantahala Wilderness, An "8" 25'
.3 of a mile, water crossing, easy

Note: The unimproved road leading to the parking area may not be passable after rains.

Directions: From the Tate Branch Campground, drive north on F.S. 70 for 2.45 miles. (There may be a dilapidated red barn on the left here.) Turn right onto an unmarked dirt road and drive .15 of a mile to the parking area.

Hike up the remainder of the driveable road and soon cross to the north side of Denton Creek. Follow the old roadbed upstream passing several jeep-blocking mounds. In .2 of a mile the road forks. Take the right fork. This road peters out into a pathway. Follow the path up Denton Creek's cove for 800' to the base of the falls.

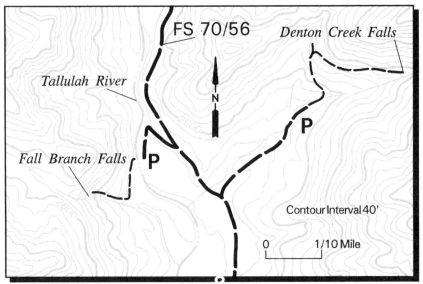

B3. Fall Branch Falls,
Towns County, Georgia

Map: Southern Nantahala Wilderness,   A "7"
.2 of a mile, potentially deep water crossing, easy-moderate
See Denton Creek Falls for hiking map.

Note: With an automobile, park on F.S. 70 and walk through the camping areas as the campground road requires high clearance.

Carry flip-flops or tennis shoes to wade the river's icy-cold waters.

Directions: From the Tate Branch Campground drive north on F.S. 70 for 2.6 miles to a single-lane road that forks left and descends to a primitive camping area 300' ahead. At this camping area the road turns sharply left to follow the Tallulah River downstream. In 200' the road ends at another camping area on the river bank. (There may be a small multi-trunked yellow birch [yellow-silver, paper-like bark] here for further verification.) Park here.

Look for a path leading 30' to the river's edge. Then look directly across the river for a small opening in the laurel. Wade the knee-deep river. (If the river is too deep here, walk upstream to the nearby island in hopes of finding a more spread out and thus shallower route across. If you use this shallower route, you'll have more rhododendron to make your way through heading downstream on the west bank.) Once across, look for a small tar-papered cabin 50' west of the river and up the hillside (this assures the correct location). Walk downstream through thick rhododendron that gives way to gradually opening woods and pass through a marshy area being reclaimed by small trees. Follow the rhododendron-lined base of the mountain and at .1 of a mile arrive at an old, barely discernable roadbed. This road turns west to follow nearby Fall Branch upstream. Hike the roadbed upstream and when it plays out continue through the rhododendron thicket to the base of this seemingly endless series of leaps and cascades.

B4. N.C. state line (as above).

B5. Bull Cove, Bear Creek, and High Falls, Clay County, N. Carolina

Map: Southern Nantahala Wilderness
Bull Cove A "7" 40', moderate
Bear Creek A "2" 20' & 50' respectively, moderate-difficult
High Falls An "8" 70'+, difficult
Beech Creek Trail #378, water crossings   See text for distances.

Note: Allow at least one-half day to see all three.

Directions: As you near 7.8 miles on the odometer look carefully for the Beech Creek Trail on the right. It may be marked with a carsonite stake, but don't count on it, as trail markers frequently disappear. Just ahead there is a circular parking area on the left that is shrouded by roadside trees. This is used mainly by people with pull behind campers and small RV's. Park here and walk the road south for 175' to the trailhead on the left. This hike is one of the more difficult in this book and shows this trait early on.

As you enter the woods, the official trail turns left to ascend the steep mountainside via three well constructed switchbacks. People have chosen to shortcut these switchbacks to the degree that the main trail goes virtually unused. (A couple of strategically placed tiger pits would solve the problem. Please use the official trail, the switchbacks are safer and easier to ascend than the straight-up-the-mountain shortcut.) After hiking .3 of a mile crest Scaly Ridge and pass through a saddle-type gap. The high mountain seen to the east from this vantage point is Little Bald. Beech Creek is heard far below.

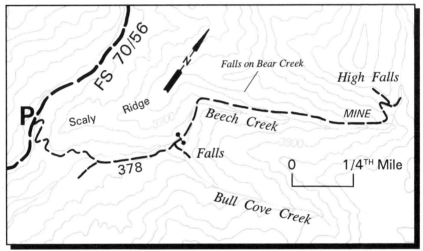

The trail runs fairly level for a little more than .1 of a mile as it gently outlines two hollows. It then descends steeply to Beech Creek. At .55 of a mile cross Beech Creek. High water levels of winter and spring make this a wet crossing unless you're lucky enough to find a log to cross on, as I was. Once across, the trail surmounts two small rises and leaves sight of the creek while passing through a stretch of boulders and young hemlock. Six tenths of a mile into the hike arrive at an old mining road which serves as the treadway for the rest of the hike. (Flag where you intersect the road, so that you'll not miss this spot on the return trip.) Hike the road upstream. With the exceptions of a couple of creek crossings, a moderate incline, and a short rocky stretch, the rest of the hike to Bull Cove Falls is easy to moderate.

At the 1 mile point, arrive at the aforementioned rocky stretch. (From this area in the winter one can see Bull Cove Falls up the creek's cove.) In 200' cross Bull Cove Creek and look for the pathway leading upstream on the north side of its cove. Duck, bob, and weave your way up the boulder- and windfall-strewn cove to the base of the falls 350' away.

The feature that stands out here is the super-looking cliffs to the north. This facet may go unnoticed while you're busy negotiating the cove. When you reach the base area look left and admire the 100'+ cliffs that sport moss where the shade allows. Still higher up, mosses give way to toadskin lichen then barren rock with jutting, shelf-like overhangs topped by hemlock. The waterfall isn't the prettiest that I've seen, but the cliffs and falls tend to compliment one another very nicely.

Return to the Beech Creek Trail and continue upstream. Shortly after passing by an iron gate the trail bends right then left as it passes by a rock wall on the right. In late summer you'll be knee-deep in pale touch-me-nots. Here, trail and creek come close together. One and two-tenths miles into the hike cross Beech Creek just below a very scenic cascade. This crossing is easily made on steppingstones in the dry months. At other times it is a wet one. From this crossing on, the going is tough, and although you're hiking an old roadbed the treadway narrows to a single track. Climb the steep, rocky grade and in another .5 of a mile pass by the lower portion of Bear Creek Falls.

This waterfall is composed of dozens of small rivulets. The upper falls lie 200' up the mountainside. They may be seen by backing away from the lower falls to the south edge of the roadbed. While standing on the eastern edge of the creek bank, align your sight over the east side of the top of the lower falls. The upper falls are found up the slope at approximately the 2 o'clock position.

Continue up the rocky trail crossing small branches and passing several scenic rock outcrops as well. At times Beech Creek is close by, then at others deep in the gorge. At 2.3 miles stop and examine the ruins of an old corundum mine on the left, whose mortarless rock walls are still partially intact.

In approximately 50' the trail turns sharply left and soon back to the right in switchback fashion. Just when you thought it couldn't get rockier—it does. The right portion of the switchback is long and steep as well. Two and six-tenths miles into the hike, where the trail turns sharply left again (the top of the first and beginning of the second switchback), look for a path on the right. There may be a sign here reading "High Falls." This pathway leads 700', steeply at times, down to the base of the falls.

At the base you'll find an island from which to view them. This is a very beautiful waterfall, 40' wide at the base and close to 70' high. Higher if you count what's not readily seen from the base. On a sunny, blue-sky day it flows as hundreds of white-water rivulets set against black rock. I am reminded of Crabtree Falls in Yancey County, N.C. (Blue Ridge Parkway), by this waterfall, only this one is larger and harder to photograph.

Some of the photo problems you'll encounter in the growing season are the high contrast of deep shade at the base with bright water and skies above. If photographing from the base you'll have deciduous trees blocking the view and problems with keystoning. A perspective control lens would be very handy here. Clear-blue skies, high water levels, and the lack of foliage in wintertime make the best photographic conditions.

B6. Thomas Falls,
Clay County, North Carolina

Map: Southern Nantahala Wilderness   A "2"
No official trail to falls, .8 of a mile, water crossings, moderate

From the jeep-blocking boulders hike north soon passing the information board and the sign "Deep Gap Trail #377." The trail ascends at an easy to moderate rate and for the most part is within sight of the Tallulah River. At 900' pass the trail register. At .3 of a mile enter a large opening. This is the site of an old homestead. The trail bends lazily through this field and reenters the woods on its north side. At .45 of a mile pass the Beech Creek Trail (#378) which splits off to the right. The Deep Gap Trail continues straight and in 70' crosses Chimney Rock Branch. The trail gracefully winds while passing through a beautiful forest then at .6 of a mile crosses a wet-weather branch. In just over 200' look for signs

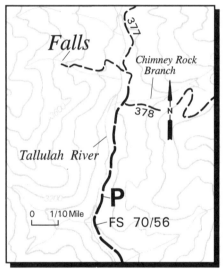

stating, "N.C. Wildlife Gamelands Boundary." Backtrack 40' and look towards the river for an overgrown, bulldozed roadbed. (Thomas Creek may be seen spilling into the river from the west at this point.) This roadbed leads in S fashion to the banks of the Tallulah River. At .65 of a mile cross the river on steppingstones. Once across, the path vanishes. Continue west and slightly upstream. Soon the rhododendron thicket gives way to more open woods. Three-hundred feet from the river look for the plainly visible scars of an old roadbed cut into the base of the hillside. Hike this roadbed south for a short distance where it then turns uphill and bends west to enter the cove of Thomas Creek. The pathway crosses to the south bank of Thomas Creek and at .8 of a mile arrives at the base of the falls.

This is a small chute-type waterfall flowing through a V in the rock. The rock's beautiful browns show through its waters. A large exposure of moss-covered bedrock flanks its north side. Although I've never visited them in summer, I believe it would be the best time to visit, account of there being no scenic backdrop when the leaves are off.

Falls on Kilby Mill Creek

Roads: Graveled   A "4" 40'
U.S.G.S. Quadrangle: Dillard, Ga.
No official trail, .25 of a mile, water crossing, easy

Directions: From U.S. 76 drive north on Persimmon Valley Road for 5.3 miles (or approximately 1 additional mile from F.S. 70) to Patterson Gap Road

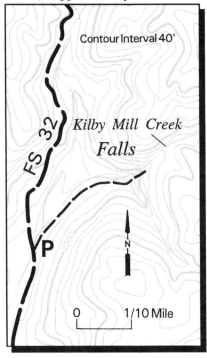

(F.S. 32). Veer left and drive 2.2 miles to the pullout on the right (just south of the bridge crossing Kilby Mill Creek). Park at the jeep-blocking mound.

Cross the jeep mound and hike an old roadbed upstream for just over .1 of a mile. Pass the confluence of Kilby Mill Creek and an unnamed branch. The pathway continues alongside the unnamed branch and soon crosses it on steppingstones. Once across, turn upstream and pick up the pathway (old roadbed) which then veers left towards the cove of Kilby Mill Creek. Pass through a stand of open woods and after hiking a total of .2 of a mile arrive at Kilby Mill Creek. A small cascade is seen here. The falls are reached by taking a tunnel-like path, on the right, through a thicket of hemlock and rhododendron. In 200' arrive at the base area.

C. Directions: From the intersection of Ga. Hwy. 197 and U.S. 76, take 197 south to the following points of interest:

C1. F.S. 165A, access to the Falls on Moccasin Creek: 3.7 miles.

C2. F.S. 26, access to the Falls on Wildcat Creek: 5.1 miles.

C3. Burton Dam Road: 8.4 miles. Drive east on Burton Dam Road for 1.6 miles to:
C3(a) The pullout for the Falls on Horse Branch. (Alternate directions: *From Bridge Creek Road drive west on Burton Dam Road for 1.3 miles to the pullout on the left.)

C1. Falls on Moccasin Creek

Roads: Dirt/High Clearance   A "5" & "10" respectively
U.S.G.S. Quadrangle: Lake Burton, Ga.
Hemlock Falls Trail,   1.6 miles,   water crossing,   easy-moderate

Note: For the novice hiker end your trek at Hemlock Falls as the upper falls require a great deal more hiking skill.

Directions: From Hwy. 197, turn right (west), across from the Moccasin Creek State Park entrance, onto F.S. 165A. (A sign on 165A announces "Lake Burton Wildlife Management Area.") Drive to the road's circular end (.6 of a mile away) and park. The trail begins at a jeep-blocking mound topped by a large stone enscribed with the words "Hemlock Falls Trail." The trail leads upstream along an old logging railroad bed to our objectives.

The trail avoids the railroad bed's initial ups and downs by treading the high ground beside it. The trail drops back to road level in .2 of a mile and passes under a canopy of rhododendron. The cascading creek and scenic trail are forced progressively closer as the drainage narrows and the mountainsides steepen. In places, trickling cascades flow off the slopes and wet the treadway. After rainfall you may encounter soggy stretches and in winter, ice. At .7 of a mile arrive at an especially scenic spot where the trail descends to cross a footbridge. (This creek crossing was once a treacherous ford. Bear this in mind if the bridge is missing.) The creek makes an S bend here among numerous white-water cascades that spill into beautiful clear-green pools.

Once across, ascend the steps and pass more cascades. In harmony with the creek, the trail bends right and continues ascending at an easy rate. At .95 of a mile the trail levels off and the bright waters of Hemlock Falls come into view. Just shy of a mile, look for a side trail that leads 100' to an open viewing area of this waterfall.

Hemlock Falls is a 10'-high tumbling waterfall that spills onto a flat bedrock slab. Its rock face is 35' wide with 12-15' of water coverage. Rhododendron overhangs the creek with hardwoods and hemlock, straight and tall, flanking its slopes. There is a large plunge pool at the base with medium-size boulders downstream.

(*See "A" Directions pg. 62 for directions to this point.)

The falls are best photographed when brightly lit by an overhead sun.
To reach the upper falls, return to the main trail and hike upstream. In 350'

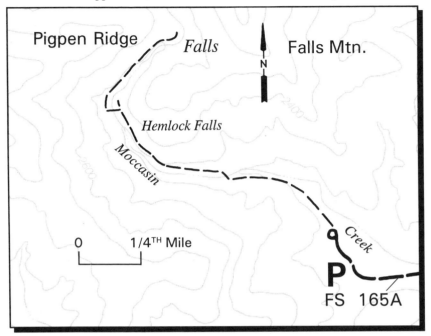

Pigpen Ridge   *Falls*   Falls Mtn.

N

Hemlock Falls

Moccasin

0   1/4TH Mile

Creek

P

FS 165A

the official trail ends beside Hemlock Falls at a sign stating "Trail not maintained for public use past this point." The *path* to the upper falls begins here and narrows significantly as it turns uphill. Just ahead (less than 100') the pathway forks. Take the lower fork and cross the creek on steppingstones. (I found a suitable crossing just across from a streamside camping area on Moccasin Creek's west bank. The old railroad bed which will serve as our path once again, is now seen on the distant hillside beyond this camping area.) Pass through the camping area and immediately go uphill to intersect the railroad bed. Again treading the railbed, the pathway steepens on the west side of the creek. At 1.15 miles the path turns steeply down into the windfall-strewn ravine of a small creek. Returning to grade level, the pathway is now high above the rush and tumble of Moccasin Creek in what I consider one of the more scenic portions of the hike.

After passing by the boulder fields of Pigpen Ridge, at 1.4 miles cross another ravine, this one with a smooth rock exposure. In 250' pass by hundreds of beautiful boulders on the left, with a small cliff topping them off. Nearing 1.5 miles the roadbed narrows into a slim pathway then again widens. At 1.6 miles arrive at a point alongside the very audible but not yet visible falls. Look for the pathway to the base just opposite a large boulder outcrop on the left.

Descend the steep (45°) pathway for approximately 80'. There, you must lower yourself 4' between two boulders to creek level.

The upper falls are one of north Georgia's most beautiful sights. They have a huge plunge pool, 50' across and 50' out from their base, with large boulders on the downstream end. The falls are 30' wide and drop 25', split in two flows. Large boulders and exposed rock flank the left side, with white pine and hemlock on the right. A solid bank of rhododendron covers the steep slope immediately above the plunge pool on the right. This is another location where I saw a hornets' nest bobbing in the breeze high above the pool.

An overcast day is best to photograph both the upper falls and the boulder field passed on the way in.

C2. Falls on Wildcat Creek

Roads: Graveled   Upper A "3"   No hiking map needed.
U.S.G.S. Quadrangles: Lake Burton, Tray Mtn., Ga. See text for distances.

Directions: From Hwy. 197 take F.S. 26 for 1.35 miles to the first falls. This waterfall, which is seen from the road, runs for 300' as a series of cascades then makes a final 15' leaping plunge.

The next feature of this creek is a sliding rock which is another .2 of a mile up the road. This natural waterslide is approximately 15' long with a small swimming hole at its base.

The upper falls are 3.8 miles from the pavement (.4 of a mile from the third bridge). Park in a pullout beside them. Walk the road downstream for 100' to the pathway leading to the base.

This is a small (8' high) but very beautiful waterfall. It is located downstream from a large primitive campground which probably accounts for the nearby litter.

C3. The intersection of Ga. Hwy. 197 and Burton Dam Road (as above).

C3(a) Falls on Horse Branch

Roads: Paved   A "6" 45'
U.S.G.S. Quadrangle: Lake Burton, Ga.
No official trail, .3 of a mile, water crossings, moderate

Note: This is a short but very rugged hike that involves crossing then walking in the creek much of the way. Windfalls and rhododendron thickets make it all the more difficult.

Directions: From Hwy. 197, drive east on Burton Dam Road for 1.6 miles. Look carefully for the pullout on the right and an old logging road that descends and enters the woods from it. There may be a large rotting oak with a red band painted around it as well. (For further identification there is a hollow on both the north and south sides of the road. A power line also crosses the road north to south here.) Park here.

Upon entering the woods the old road descends at a moderate rate and in 200' crosses a small branch. Turning uphill, passing over windfalls and through

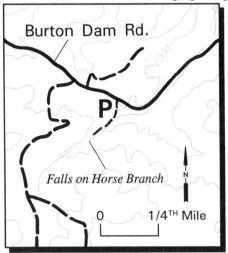

Burton Dam Rd.

P

Falls on Horse Branch

N

0   1/4ᵀᴴ Mile

rhododendron thickets, in 800' the road plays out. From here on you must hike in and out of the creek. After hiking a total of .3 of a mile you'll find the falls hidden in an alcove on the right.

Located in a cirque-like area with stratified-rock cliffs of 60-70', hemlocks tower 200' above the viewpoint. The falls drop from a ledge a sheer 45' and splash onto flat bedrock before spilling over a bedrock staircase. The rock wall on the left side weeps nutrients to hundreds of aquatic plants.

Clarkesville - Cornelia Area

Nancytown Falls, Habersham County, Georgia

Roads: Graveled   A "2" 20'
U.S.G.S. Quadrangle: Ayersville, Ga.
Sourwood Trail #155, blue blazed, minor water crossings, easy

Note: Best seen after rainfall.

F.S. 92 is shown on the official map as being F.S. 61.

Directions: From U.S. 23/441 take the Mt. Airy - Clarkesville exit (Old Hwy. 197, sign: Lake Russell Recreation Area). Travel south on Old 197 and soon pass a sign: "Lake Russell 6 miles." At the second stop sign intersect Dick's Hill Parkway (Old U.S. 123). Turn left and drive .2 of a mile to Nancytown Road. Turn right and cross the bridge over the railroad tracks. In .1 of a mile the road turns right (retaining its name) as it is intersected by Welcome Home Road from the left. Continue for a total of .5 of a mile to the Forest Service boundary (gate) at the end of the pavement. (Park on the right if the road [F.S. 92] is gated.)

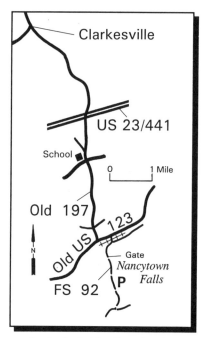

Hike or drive an additional .75 of a mile to a point where the Sourwood Trail crosses the road. Park here.

Marked by a carsonite stake, the trail enters the woods on the east side of F.S. 92 and leads up a rise for approximately 200'. The trail then descends at a moderate rate and outlines a hollow while passing through an open stand of hardwoods. At the quarter-mile point the trail turns sharply left and crosses a small branch on a footbridge. The trail now turns uphill to ascend a small ridge. Descending its east slope the trail bends left then meanders through the hardwoods and sparse pines. At .35 of a mile the trail bends right and crosses a small branch in a very scenic area of streamside laurel. After this second stream crossing the trail is fairly level as it parallels the nearby creek. At the half-mile point the trail tops a small ridge line (the falls can be heard from this rise when the leaves are off), bends left, and descends steeply into an

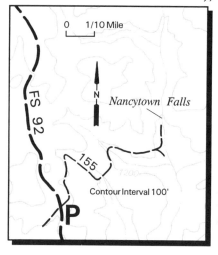

area with a marsh on the right and Nancytown Creek flowing into it from the left. At .55 of a mile arrive at a trail sign pointing right, for the Sourwood Loop Trail, and left, to the falls. (In winter the falls may be seen up the cove on the left from this trail intersection.) The trail now parallels Nancytown Creek upstream as it flows between laurel-covered hillsides dotted with short leaf pine and hardwoods. At just over .6 of a mile, among large beech trees, arrive at the base of this sliding-type waterfall.

Clayton South

Panther Creek Recreation Area, Habersham County, Georgia

Roads: Paved   A "5"
U.S.G.S. Quadrangle: Tallulah Falls, Ga.
Trail #72, blue blazed, 6.0 miles, water crossings, moderate

Note: Rains in the summer of '94 washed out many of the footbridges along this trail. Hopefully, you'll find them replaced. The first crossing of Panther Creek at 1.4 miles is not too tricky under normal conditions. The crossing at 5.6 miles, however, is a different story. The creek is wide, deep, and crossed on slick bedrock.

The midsection of the Panther Creek Trail is especially scenic. If you plan to hike the trail's entire length, arrange for a shuttle car on the downstream end.

Directions: If driving from Clayton, take U.S. 23/441 south to the community of Tallulah Falls. Check your mileage from the Tallulah Gorge Bridge. Drive south on 23/441 for 2.3 miles then turn right onto Old 441 and travel another 1.5 miles to the parking area.

If driving north (from Clarkesville) on U.S. 23/441 take Glenn Hardman Road (the Turnerville exit) north, signs: "Panther Creek Recreation Area." In .1 of a mile intersect Old 441. Turn right (north) and drive 1 mile to trail parking.

Shuttle directions: From the intersection of Ga. Hwys. 17 and 184 in Toccoa, drive north on 184 (Prather Bridge Road) for 6.0 miles. Veer left onto a paved road leading to Yonah Lake and Dam. After traveling 5.1 miles turn left onto F.S. 182 (a dirt road). Drive the often muddy road for 1.6 miles to the eastern terminus of the Panther Creek Trail.

The trail enters the woods on the east side of Old 441, just north of the creek. (An old roadbed leads uphill here while the trail is closest to the creek.) At 220' exit the woods and enter the right of way on the west side of U.S. 441. Pass under the U.S. 441 bridges and reenter the National Forest. Soon the sounds of the highway dissipate. At one third of a mile the trail turns right and leaves the drier slopes, heading closer to the creek. For much of its entire length the trail is a meandering and undulating one that sometimes leaves sight and sound of the creek. Nearing the half-mile point cross a small branch and soon thereafter pass under power lines. The trail levels out on a roadbed for a short distance and regains sight of the creek. The next landmarks are red painted bearing trees and a survey marker at .75 of a mile, followed by a large rock overhang at .9 of a mile. At 1.05 miles double blue-blazes call attention to a potentially confusing left turn. The trail appears to continue straight ahead but in fact switchbacks to climb through a split in the boulders while passing a series of noisy cascades. The trail is root-laced and rocky in this vicinity. Panther Creek is obscured from view in many areas here by the thick laurel and rhododendron. At 1.35 miles the trail leaves the hillsides and heads for the creek bottom.

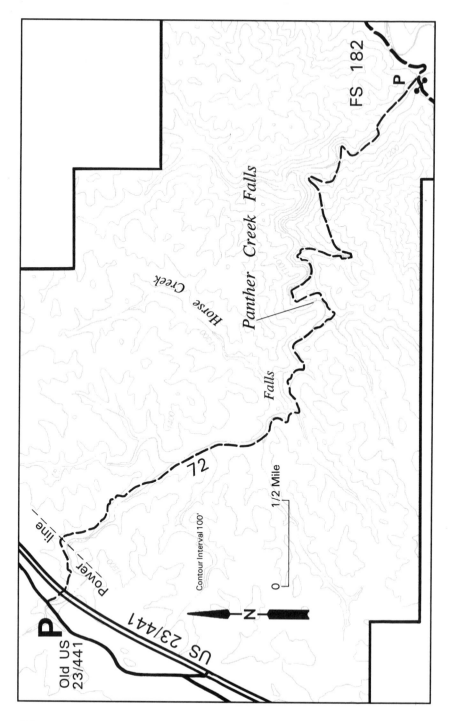

FS 182

P

Panther Creek Falls

Horse Creek

Falls

72

Contour Interval 100'

1/2 Mile

0

N

Power line

P

Old US 23/441

US 23/441

At 1.4 miles cross to the south side of Panther Creek where a footbridge once stood. For the next mile, much of it on an old logging road, the trail is in the creek bottom, crossing several small creeks while treading more level ground. At just over 2.3 miles arrive at a small viewing area atop the upper falls. The trail makes a reverse S and descends the height of the falls to creek level where a side path leads to the base for better viewing.

Running for 70' with a cascading drop of 15', this waterfall is set among some of the area's most scenic rock.

Continuing downstream, for the most part the trail remains in the creek bottom and crosses small tributaries. At 2.8 miles reach the first of many rock outcrops whose exposed cliffs are protected by cables serving as handrails. (These exposures become more numerous as you near the lower falls.) Between 2.8 and 3.25 miles the trail is much easier, treading in the relatively flat creek bottom. At 3.4 miles pass an unmarked side trail that leads south. Hearts a bustin' (euonymus), club moss, partridgeberry, ferns, and galax abound in this area.

At 3.5 miles arrive at the top of Panther Creek Falls. The falls run for 300 to 400', falling in three major stages. Two narrow and smaller tiers precede the much higher and wider lower tier. Use caution if venturing to the top of the lower tier: the bedrock may be slick from spray and in winter, glazed with ice. Seen on the creek's north side is rock that has been worn smooth over the ages.

Cables again protect the trail as it switchbacks down alongside the falls. At 3.55 miles arrive at a wide and sandy beach-like area used by campers at the base of the falls.

The lower tier is 30' high and 30' wide with a large pool as well as a large exposure of granite. (You may want to end your hike here, unless you have a shuttle car in place on the trail's downstream end.)

From Panther Creek Falls the trail continues downstream closely following the creek before becoming more woods oriented. It also becomes more rugged with plenty of rocks, roots, and things to duck. Four miles into the hike, reach the midpoint of another reverse S bend with large granite boulders in the creek. Still further downstream are more of these boulders and a rushing cascade.

At 4.15 miles the trail is protected by cables and makes a hard right at double blue-blazes. After ascending at a moderate rate with Panther Creek approximately 100' in elevation below, at 4.2 miles leave its sight as you enter the hollow of a small tumbling creek. Following this creek's west bank upstream, the trail switchbacks, treads wooden structures, then at 4.4 miles crosses the creek on a footbridge. The trail ascends the south side of a knob steeply and bends left while rounding its slope. After passing through a saddle-type gap cloaked in pines the trail descends steeply and outlines a hollow. The sound of Panther Creek which has not been present for the last 2000' returns, and it is now seen approximately 200' in elevation below. At 5.1 miles arrive at a point where the galax-lined trail is somewhat open and shifted to the north side of the ridge. The hillsides are steep on both sides of the creek. The trail makes a sharp right and runs along the foot of a ridge line. The hardwood forest carries a sweet, almost cedar-like scent from the interspersed hemlock. At 5.25 miles cross another footbridge in the hollow of a small trickling branch then pass an exposure protected by cables. In this area the trail undulates through a couple of hollows while losing elevation. At 5.45 miles cross a hollow on a footbridge then descend to Panther Creek. With a small island just upstream, look for blue blazes and the piers of a washed-out footbridge. Cross to the east side of Panther Creek. A sign where the bridge once stood states "Panther Creek Trail," with distances given for upstream travel. At 5.6 miles arrive at the official trail ending.

American holly, small hemlocks, and partridgeberry are present in the creek bottom. In this wide and sandy bottom, numerous logs have washed downstream and snagged on their living counterparts. In the next .2 of a mile there are large boulders strewn about the woodland and rounded stones fill the creek. At 5.85 miles descend, then cross a small tributary. The Panther Creek Trail exits the woods on a sandy roadbed that parallels the north side of the creek. On the approach to the parking area pass a jeep ford which is gated on the creek's south side. The hike ends at a turnaround-type parking area (a total of 6.0 miles).

Clayton - Dillard Area

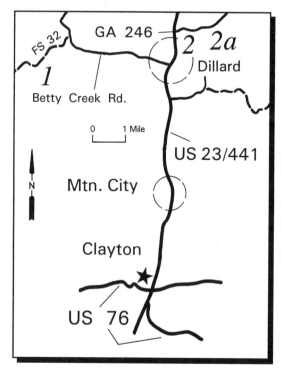

Directions: From the intersection of U.S. 441 and U.S. 76 West in Clayton, drive north on 441 the following distances to these points of interest:

1. Betty Creek Road (access to Laurel Mountain Falls): 6.75 miles.
2. The intersection of U.S. 441 and Ga. Hwy. 246: 7.75 miles. Take 246 east to:
2(a) Estatoah Falls: .9 of a mile.

1. Laurel Mountain Falls, Rabun County, Georgia

Roads: Graveled A "5" No hiking map needed.
U.S.G.S. Quadrangle: Dillard, Ga.
No official trail, 300', easy-difficult

Directions: From U.S. 441 in Dillard, turn left (west) onto Betty Creek Road. The Valley Volunteer Fire Department is on the left at this location. Drive Betty Creek Road for 3.5 miles to Patterson Gap Road (F.S. 32, sign: "Moon Valley Resort"). Turn left, after crossing a bridge the pavement gives way to gravel. Drive .5 of a mile up the mountainside to the pullout on the right. Park here. (There is a 4-WD road on the right that enters the woods at a 90° angle at this location.) You can hear the falls across the road (on your left) and down below.

Cross the road and enter the woods on a descending pathway. In approximately 40' arrive creekside. The first cascade (and prettiest in my opinion) is just upstream. Patterson Creek tumbles down the steep-sided gorge as a series of cataracts. An exploratory path leads steeply alongside the creek for another 300' to their base.

2. The intersection of U.S. 441 and Ga. Hwy. 246 (as above).

2(a) Estatoah Falls, Rabun County, Georgia

This waterfall is located on private property. It may be seen from Ga. Hwy. 246 as you top a rise .9 of a mile from U.S. 441. The high water levels of winter and spring offer the best viewing. In summer and fall they're a mere trickle.

Please, no trespassing!

Clayton East

To simplify driving directions the text for this area is broken into two sections: "A" and "B" (the route map, however, is shared). All directions contained herein will originate at either "A" or "B". All of the waterfalls listed in this section are located in Rabun County.

Directions: At the traffic light on U.S. 441 in Clayton, where U.S. 76 goes west, turn *east* onto Rickman St. and in .5 of a mile intersect Warwoman Road at a stop sign. This stop sign intersection is point "A."

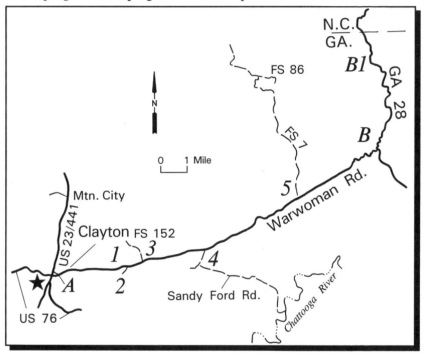

A. "A" (described above) provides access to the waterfalls along Warwoman Road (check your mileage from this point).

B. "B" is the intersection of Warwoman Road and Ga. Hwy. 28. It is reached by taking Warwoman Road east for 13.7 miles from point "A." (Text for the waterfalls listed under "B" begins on pg. 87.)

A. Directions: From the intersection described above, drive east on Warwoman Road the following distances to:

1. Becky Branch Fall's parking area: 2.15 miles.
2. The Falls in The Warwoman Dell Recreation Area: 2.4 miles.

3. Finney Creek Road (F.S. 152), access to Martin Creek Falls: 3.0 miles.
4. Sandy Ford Road, access to the Falls on Dicks Creek: 5.35 miles.
5. Hale Ridge Road (F.S. 7), access to Holcomb and Ammons Creek Falls: 9.65 miles.

1. Becky Branch Falls, Loop Trail

Roads: Paved   A "4" 20'
U.S.G.S. Quadrangle: Rabun Bald, Ga.
BT, .2 of a mile round trip, 10 minutes, moderate-difficult

At this location look for a bronze historic marker, on the right, which is dedicated to explorer-botanist William Bartram. (The Bartram Trail crosses

Warwoman Road here.) There are pullouts on both sides of the road for parking.

Hike the Bartram Trail (on the north side of Warwoman Road) up the left side of the cove. Take your time up the steep grade and enjoy the scenery of this small but rugged gorge. In 375' pass a small concrete block building. Continue another 140' to the bridge at the base of the falls.

With adequate rainfall this is a beautiful tumbling waterfall. On a spring visit you'll encounter Jack-in-the-pulpit in the fall's moist environs.

Hike the east side of the cove to complete the loop. The Bartram Trail soon splits off to the left. There are spots along the return trail that offer parting views of the falls. At 800' the loop switchbacks down the steep mountainside. I saw my first yellow fringed orchid on this drier slope. In another 300' arrive back at the parking area.

2. Falls in The Warwoman Dell Recreation Area

Roads: Paved   A "3" 12'   See Becky Branch Falls for hiking map.
U.S.G.S. Quadrangle: Rabun Bald, Ga.
Self-Guiding Loop Trail, .4 of a mile total, easy

Note: The road to the recreation area is gated in winter.

Directions: From the Becky Branch pullout, continue east on Warwoman Road for .2 of a mile to the recreation area entrance. Turn right. Park in the pavillion parking lot .25 of a mile ahead.

Winter access: Park at the Becky Branch parking area and hike the Bartram Trail south as it switchbacks into Warwoman Dell. In 400' intersect the road for the Warwoman Dell Picnic Area. Hike this road west to the parking area.

Look for the trailhead (marked with a carsonite stake) and leaflet holder at the northwest corner of the parking lot. This nature trail has numbered stops keyed to the leaflet telling of the local flora and fauna.

Upon entering the woods the trail parallels a small creek. In 100' the treadway turns left, slightly away from the creek, and ascends towards the pavillion. At 300', in the vicinity of the pavillion, turn right and cross a footbridge. The loop trail begins and ends here. Hiking in a counterclockwise direction, pass through a small picnic area. The trail then turns left and up the hill as it reenters the woods. At 900' cross a small branch on a footbridge. I spotted the poisonous white baneberry in this area. This rare and interesting plant is commonly known as doll's eyes for its white berries which resemble the china eyes once used in doll making. At .2 of a mile reach the apex of the loop. A narrow side trail on the right leads 50' to the base of Warwoman Falls.

Set on the north-facing slope of a deeply-shaded 20' ravine, this waterfall and the adjacent cliffs receive very little sunlight. This makes it tough to photograph with small apertures and slow films. Of particular beauty are the moss-covered cliffs and the gnarled roots of trees that have managed a toehold here.

Return to the main trail and continue in a counterclockwise direction. At .25 of a mile cross a small footbridge and take the trail uphill. Top a rise then drop back down and rejoin the fall's branch. At .35 of a mile intersect the entrance portion of the trail at the above mentioned picnic area.

3. Martin Creek Falls

Roads: Graveled   A "7"   See Becky Branch Falls for hiking map.
U.S.G.S. Quadrangle: Rabun Bald, Ga.
BT, .5 of a mile, 20 minutes, water crossing, easy-moderate

Directions: From Warwoman Road, turn left onto Finney Creek Road (F.S. 152) and soon pass the Game Checking Station. One-half mile from the pavement, in a sharp bend to the left, look for a primitive camping area on the left. Park here.

Hike through this camping area then bear slightly right and pass through the cut-up windfalls. At 200' pass through another camping area then bear left and take the slim path leading to Martin Creek. At 340', being very careful, cross the creek on slick steppingstones. (After rainfall you may get your feet wet here.) The path then bends right as it climbs steeply for .1 of a mile to intersect the Bartram Trail. Hike the Bartram Trail upstream, passing several mini falls and cascades in a steep-sided sluice. This sluice has beautiful water-sculpted swirlholes in its moss-covered granite. Cross a small tributary and as you near .3 of a mile pass through an open stand of woods used by campers. Slightly more than .4 of a mile into the hike cross another small branch whereupon the Bartram Trail turns uphill. In approximately 100' arrive at a side trail leading to the base of the falls.

This two-tier waterfall is 35' high with aquatic plants covering the weeping rock wall on the left.

This location photographs best under diffused lighting.

4. Falls on Dicks Creek

Roads: Graveled   An "8" 50'
U.S.G.S. Quadrangle: Whetstone, Ga., S.C.
BT/CRT, .5 of a mile, 15 minutes, easy

Directions: From Warwoman Road, turn right onto Sandy Ford Road (a paved road that soon gives way to gravel). In less than .1 of a mile turn right again. At .65 of a mile turn left crossing Warwoman Creek. This is Dicks Creek Road (also

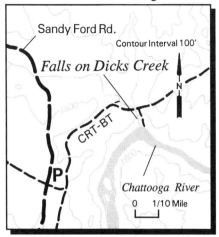

known as Sandy Ford Road). Pool Creek Road soon intersects on the right. Stay to the left. Ford a small creek at approximately 2.9 miles, then Dicks Creek at 4.0 miles (this second ford may be impassable after rainfall). Continue for a total of 4.3 miles to the parking area which is on the left. Walk the road for an additional 200' to a point where the Bartram Trail crosses.

Enter the woods on the left (east) side of the road. In 300' the yellow-blazed Chattooga River Trail intersects the Bartram Trail from the right. (This junction may go unnoticed as it is not marked.) Continuing east, the now combined trail (which is blazed with the aluminum diamond of the Bartram Trail) descends slightly and passes through a middle-aged forest of hemlock, white pine, and mixed hardwoods. At .3 of a mile the trail bottoms out in a vale. After ascending a small rise Dicks Creek comes into view. The trail descends slightly and bends sharply right to parallel the creek downstream. (From the worn track leading straight ahead to the creek, it appears that many people are confused at this spot and attempt to cross the creek, not knowing that only a short distance downstream lies the key to dry feet—a footbridge.) At .35 of a mile cross the footbridge and pass through trailside ferns and club moss. One hundred and twenty feet from the bridge, leave the Bartram Trail by taking the trail on the right. This immediately crosses a small tributary on a footbridge and parallels Dicks Creek for .1 of a mile to the top of the falls.

At the top is a panoramic view of the Dicks Creek Ledge. This is a beautiful 6' drop covering the width of the Chattooga River. (The midstream shoals are a favorite rest stop for river runners.)

Hike downstream another 300' to an obscure pathway leading to the base of the falls and a much better view of them and this scenic river.

5. Holcomb and Ammons Creek Falls

Roads: Graveled   A "10" & "7" respectively
U.S.G.S. Quadrangle: Rabun Bald, Ga.
.3 & .55 of a mile respectively, moderate
Full loop 1.7 miles, difficult

Directions: From Warwoman Road turn left (north) onto Hale Ridge Road (F.S. 7). Drive 6.8 miles to the intersection of F.S. 86. The trailhead is straight ahead. The parking area is 50' to the right (east) of the intersection.

Hike the switchbacks which lead steeply down to Holcomb Creek and enter the land of the giants. There are mature hemlocks and poplar up these coves that are among the largest I've seen—three feet in diameter for starters. The trail then turns west to follow the creek upstream to some of the finest sights in the area. After hiking .3 of a mile arrive at the bridge from which Holcomb Creek Falls are seen.

The falls are more than 100' high with boulders the size of automobiles strewn at its lower levels. There are hemlocks and pines atop it that seem to touch the sky. The water in its pools has a beautiful blue-green tint—colors borrowed from streamside laurel and rhododendron.

Cross the bridge at Holcomb Creek and pass over a small ridge. This ridge separates the Holcomb and Ammons Creek coves. In just under .2 of a mile reach a trail on the left. (This steep trail is the return portion of the loop, see hiking directions below*.) From the trail intersection continue straight ahead for 130'

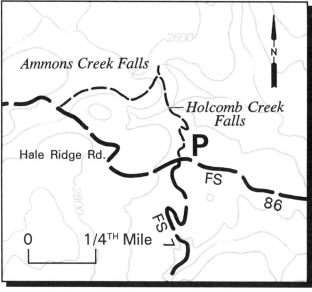

to the Ammons' Creek observation deck at the base of the falls.

Ammons Creek falls 40' over a rock face which divides its flow in half. The observation deck offers an open view of the steep gorge and tree line 200' above. A terraced, aquatic rock garden of sorts thrives on the deeply-shaded left side.

Brown salamanders lie camouflaged against the dark, moist rock.

*To complete the loop, backtrack 130' and take the return trail. This steep, narrow trail ascends Holcomb Creek's cove, initially through a tunnel-like canopy of laurel. In 600' pass by a deeply-shaded rock wall some 30 to 40' high, which is cloaked in mosses. Still ascending, the canopy opens as the trail passes a series of cascades and falls below. In just over .2 of a mile pass by one of the larger maple trees you'll encounter—18" in diameter. Approaching .3 of a mile the trail moderates somewhat and passes through the first stretches of knee-high vegetation. (There is much more of this to come.) At .45 of a mile look left for a side path that leads to a bedrock viewing area of a small (10 to 12') sliding-type waterfall. For the next .1 of a mile Holcomb Creek is a series of rushing cascades which then give way to a lazy-flowing creek. Finally, the trail levels as you approach Hale Ridge Road which is another .1 of a mile away. Hike the road in an easterly direction (towards the concrete bridge), in .6 of a mile arrive back at the parking area.

B. Directions: From the intersection of Warwoman Road and Ga. Hwy. 28, drive north on Hwy. 28 the following distance to the point listed below:

B1. The parking area on Hwy. 28 and trailhead for the Falls on Big and Overflow Creeks (Three Forks Area): 4.5 miles.

B1. Three Forks Area, Chattooga Wild and Scenic River (West Fork, Chattooga River)

This area is one of my favorites. If you want solitude you'll find it here. I usually hike during the week and have only encountered one small group of hikers on these trails.

A person of average hiking abilities should be able to see both of these locations in a day's time.

These waterfalls are located within the Chattooga Wild and Scenic River corridor. It is truly wild and scenic. Big, Holcomb, and Overflow Creeks rush, tumble, and fall from distant mountains then converge at Three Forks to form the West Fork of the Chattooga River.

It took me three attempts to reach Overflow Falls. I had read and heard about them, but no one I consulted could tell me how to *get* to them. I tried to reach them, with no success, from the west via John Teague Gap as an old book of mine suggested. Next, I hiked all the way to Three Forks and tried venturing up Overflow Creek. That didn't work either, the creek was too deep, the laurel too thick, and the mountainsides too steep. Frustrated, I gave up and headed for my truck which was parked on Hwy. 28. As I returned to the jeep mound at Salt Log Knob, I noticed a trail venturing west. It was shown on the quadrangle, so I tried it. Much to my surprise, I had finally found this elusive and most beautiful spot. For me it was ample reward for all of the hardship I had endured.

Falls on Big Creek

Roads: Paved   A "10" 30'
U.S.G.S. Quadrangle: Satolah, Ga., S.C., N.C.
Three Forks Trail,   2.2 miles,   water crossings,   difficult

---

Note: I have visited this waterfall many times. During periods of normal rainfall its one of the most beautiful that I've seen. If drought conditions exist hold off and see them another time as they are not as spectacular.

Follow the jeep ruts west from the parking area and in 200' cross Talley Mill Creek on steppingstones. (In the winter and spring you may get your feet wet here. This is the only major water crossing on this hike.) The road (F.S. 650) which serves as our trail now enters the woods and turns sharply left then passes by jeep-blocking mounds. In just over .2 of a mile pass a road on the right which leads to an area of recent logging activity. Seven tenths of a mile from the parking area pass by jeep-blocking boulders. The road (trail) undulates from here. In another .6 of a mile (1.4 miles total), in a sharp bend to the right, arrive at a path on the *left* which leads to Big Creek. This is the first path on the left and is hard to miss as it starts out wide and clear. (For further verification look for a faint roadbed 25' ahead that leads north off the Three Forks Trail.) The Three Forks Trail continues straight ahead here*.

(*See the Falls on Overflow Creek pg. 90.)

Turn left (south) and hike the path which follows an old logging road downhill. The further you go, the narrower this path gets. In .3 of a mile arrive at a very tranquil Big Creek. Hike downstream and in another .4 of a mile arrive at the Chattooga Wild and Scenic River boundary. This is denoted by blue painted trees. The falls can be heard in this area. In approximately 300' arrive near the top. The path is

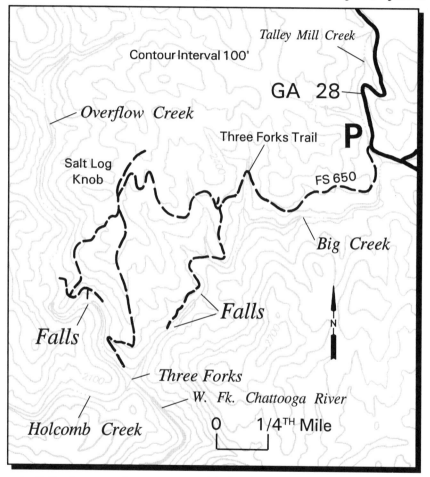

potentially dangerous here as you could slide into the creek. Have your hands free and don't venture too close. In this vicinity look carefully for the correct route that leads up and over a dead-end bluff (away from the falls). After circumventing this obstacle, make your way down the steep slope to the base area.

Seen under normal conditions this is a very powerful waterfall that photographs best with the afternoon sun brightly lighting *it* and the surrounding rock walls. Use a fast shutter speed to freeze the action and show its great power.

Falls on Overflow Creek

U.S.G.S. Quadrangle: Satolah, Ga., S.C., N.C.   A "10" 15'
3.2 miles from parking (1.8 miles from Big Creek turnoff), difficult
Hiking map shared with Falls on Big Creek.

Note: Overflow Falls is not for the fainthearted. The hike is a moderate one over undulating terrain for the first 2.4 miles, then descends steeply in its final .8 of a mile. This last .8 of a mile makes for an arduous trek on the way out.

I have visited Overflow Falls in both winter and summer. I prefer winter—the water level was nearly twice that of summer and the cooler weather was more comfortable to hike in.

*From the intersection of the Three Forks Trail and the pathway leading to Big Creek, continue west on the Three Forks Trail. In slightly less than 1 mile pass a pathway which intersects from the right. In another .1 of a mile arrive at Salt Log Knob and the Chattooga Wild and Scenic River boundary (blue painted trees). Just ahead is a very large jeep-blocking mound and pit which has standing water year-round. The trail to Overflow Falls is on the *right* here. (The Three Forks Trail continues straight ahead very steeply, leading down to the confluence of Big, Holcomb, and Overflow Creeks approximately 1 mile away.)

To reach the falls, hike the steeply descending trail for .6 of a mile to a spot where the trail turns 90° to the right. (A diversion channel has been cut in the roadway here to minimize washing.) Look carefully for the narrow pathway, on the *left*, that leads to the falls. This path is easily missed, but soon becomes easier to discern as it treads upon an overgrown logging road. The pathway then leaves the logging road with a right turn and heads down a hollow. Two tenths of a mile from the diversion channel arrive at the top of the falls.

To reach the base, look for a path just to the left of the fall's cliff. This leads the final 100' to the base.

The falls are located at the beginning of a bend with a great view of the creek upstream. The fall's cliff is laced with swirlholes and its plunge pool (known locally as the "Eel Pool," because the falls limit the upstream migration of native eels) is very large and deep. Downstream, the creek cascades into a rocky bend and out of sight on its way to Three Forks.

(*See the Falls on Big Creek pg. 88 for directions to this point.)

Falls of the Cumberland Plateau

The sandstones, shales, and limestones of this area were laid down during the Paleozoic Era, 340 to 280 million years ago, when the area was a river delta or part of an ocean floor. The land was then uplifted by plate tectonics and in the process, fissured. Streams draining through these fissures cut the canyons and "Gulfs" (as some of these canyons are known regionally) we now see. Where softer sandstones and shales were chemically or physically eroded out from under more resistant rock layers, caprock ledges remain along with the waterfalls of today. Where water penetrates and erodes the underlying limestone, caves and sinkholes are forming.

Caprock-type waterfalls are born of the following: chemical weathering and mechanical weathering. Chemical weathering is the process of water borne plant and animal acids acting to dissolve the softer underlying rock. Mechanical weathering is where the hydraulic forces of falling water and the abrasives carried by it, scour out the softer underlying rock to form alcoves and amphitheaters. Water in the form of ice also qualifies under this heading. When too much of the supporting rock (shale in most cases) is removed from under the capstone, the capstone breaks off where vertically fractured and falls in large chunks into these gulfs. With more surface area now exposed, the amphitheater and the individual rock's disintegration is further hastened.

The waterfalls of the T.A.G. region, where Tennessee, Alabama, and Georgia meet, lie on the Cumberland Plateau and have the common trait of being of the caprock variety. Some of this area's more unusual waterfalls flow out of limestone caves and plunge into sinkholes. Alabama's Little River has the distinction of being the only river in America to run its entire length atop a mountain (Lookout Mountain, a part of the Cumberland Plateau itself).

Remember, to see them at their best ...go when they flow! For the falls of the Cumberland Plateau this means winter and spring when rainfall is adequate and the water table is up.

Spanning many creeks in Tennessee's State Parks and Natural Areas are some of the finest suspension footbridges that you'll ever set foot on. The views from these lofty spans are truly incredible. If you're acrophobic or prone to sea sickness you probably won't get the thrill or enjoy the sights as much as I did while crossing them. Remember, no more than two persons at a time on these bridges, please!

Desoto State Park and
Little River Canyon National Preserve

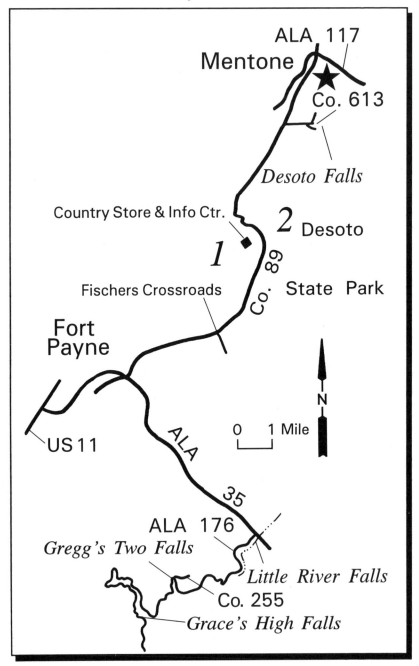

ALA 117

Mentone

Co. 613

Desoto Falls

Country Store & Info Ctr.

1

2 Desoto

Co. 89

Fischers Crossroads

State Park

Fort
Payne

N

0   1 Mile

US 11

ALA

35

ALA 176

Gregg's Two Falls

Little River Falls

Co. 255

Grace's High Falls

Desoto State Park is named for Spanish explorer, Hernando Desoto, whose party is thought to have traveled through the area in the 1540's. The park and its neighbor to the south, Little River Canyon, sit atop Lookout Mountain which in my opinion is one of the most beautiful regions in the east. Please help keep it that way by living up to their cleverly adapted motto ... "Take only pictures, leave only footprints, kill only time."

Next in line to waterfalls I like canyons best. This area offers both. I've visited many of the canyon country national parks and monuments of the Desert Southwest. Little River Canyon reminds me of Walnut Canyon, Arizona, with two major differences—water, and a lush deciduous forest. Both canyons have been carved into sand and limestones of similar origin and color. You won't find the desert bighorn here, but you will see turkey, deer, and well-fed chipmunks sporting potbellies.

The Little River is the only river in America that originates and runs its entire length atop a mountain. Born near the point where the Alabama and Georgia state line bisects the Tennessee line, the river has carved a canyon into Lookout Mountain that is some 16 miles long and three fourths of a mile across at its widest point. With an average depth of 400' and maximum depth of 700', Little River Canyon is considered the deepest canyon east of the Mississippi. On the canyon's north end are 100-200' sheer sandstone cliffs and numerous long-distance vistas. As you drive south the cliffs give way to a wide valley between sloping mountains.

On my first visit (in the fall of the year), the waterfalls were disappointing, as water levels were down. However, I found their rock alcoves so beautiful that I knew they would be truly awesome after a good soaking rain. Wanting to see them at their best, I hit the road just two weeks later as a cold front was pushing clouds out that had provided a steady but adequate 2" rain to the area.

The Little River, which only two weeks before filled one fourth of the rocky riverbed, now filled its full width with raging waters. Grace's High Falls, which were dry on my previous visit, were now flowing full bore. Along the rim were dozens of wet-weather waterfalls spilling into the canyon. The creeks and rivers of the Cumberland Plateau rise and recede very rapidly.

Along the rim drive are many overlooks from which beautiful views are to be had, but I think none better than the postcard setting present at Wolf Creek Overlook. The river, seen far below, is dotted with huge boulders that tumbled from the distant cliffs eons ago. On a clear-blue sky day you can see for miles, both up and downstream.

Cedar and twisted scrub pine frame most every angle. A park ranger told me that ice storms act to shape many of these trees by bending or breaking limbs which then heal in deformed shapes. In perhaps hundreds of locations along the rim, trees grow so close to the cliffs that their trunks have become grossly scarred by the rocking action of the wind. In many cases they appear to be fused with the rock.

93

There are two side canyons along the rim drive that house waterfalls; Wolf and Bear Creek Canyons. Wolf Creek Canyon is the home of Gregg's Two Falls. Grace's High Falls call Bear Creek Canyon home.

Unless otherwise noted, the waterfalls listed below are located in Dekalb County, Alabama.

Desoto State Park

Desoto Falls

Roads: Paved   A "10" 104'   No hiking map needed.
Map: handout at visitor center
Easy because of its short distance.

Directions: From the intersection of Ala. Hwy. 117 and Dekalb County Hwy. 89 in Mentone, drive south on 89 for 2.2 miles to County Road 613 (stop sign). Turn left and drive 1.1 miles to its end at the Desoto Fall's parking area.

Desoto Falls Lake and the A.A. Miller Dam are seen here. This dam was built in 1925 and provided the first hydro-electric power to north Alabama. The dam itself forms a very scenic man-made waterfall when adequate water flows over its top. A constant earth-trembling roar is heard and felt while standing near either the dam or falls when in full flow.

Hike downstream passing the upper cascading falls en route to the lower falls which are 350' from the parking area.

This is one of the largest waterfalls in this book: not in terms of water volume, but in terms of what water has done to shape the land. Over the centuries running water and its chemical and mechanical actions have hollowed out a huge half-circle alcove with cliffs in excess of 100'. These cliffs have a copper color similar to those of Linville Falls, N.C., only here you'll find rich shades of brown, rust, and white in addition. Huge too, is a seemingly bottomless plunge pool that measures 250' wide, extending 300' out from the cliffs. Stunted scrub pine and colorful wildflowers have colonized the clifftops and fissures where enough soil has collected to sustain life. This is a most stunning example of a caprock waterfall.

1. Lost Falls - Laurel Falls

Map: Desoto State Park
Loop 2.9 miles, minor water crossings, moderate

Note: This and the other falls in the area need adequate rainfall to be more than a trickle. Remember!...go when they flow!

Directions: From the Desoto State Park country store and information center, drive south for .15 of a mile to the parking area for the Azalea Cascade Trail. If the sign is missing, this is the *second* parking area on the right. (This parking area is also used to access Indian and Lodge Falls. See pg. 96.)

This hike makes a clockwise loop out of the Azalea Cascade, C.R. Caves, and Lost Falls Trails. Along this route you'll take in two waterfalls and some of the finest woodland scenery the park has to offer.

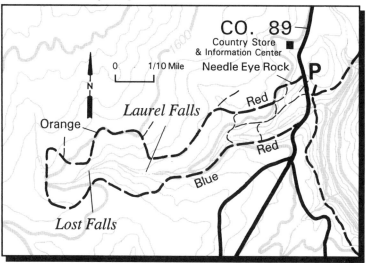

Enter the woods on the *south* side of Laurel Creek. This is the south portion of the red-blazed Azalea Cascade Trail. With galax at your feet and large trees overhead the trail begins to climb. After a bend to the right, encounter a Y intersection at .15 of a mile. A side trail here leads down to a footbridge where the scenic Azalea Cascade and its pool are viewed. (This connects with the "B" portion of the Azalea Cascade Trail in 180'.) Continuing, pass by outcrops of sandstone covered in emerald-green mosses. At .25 of a mile the blue-blazed C.R. Caves Trail (named for a former park ranger, not associated with any caverns) begins on the left, while the Azalea Cascade Trail leads to the right.

Take the meandering and undulating C.R. Caves Trail and pass by beautiful rock outcrops, some with overhangs of 15'. Hickory, maple, black and chestnut oaks, pine, poplar, and sassafras comprise the forest as you leave the wetter creek bottom. At .55 of a mile the boulders play out. The trail levels here and the woods are more open and youthful. The trail makes a right turn then treads across an area of exposed bedrock at .65 of a mile. Runoff from the exposed rock forms a small trickling branch. Large colonies of moss and lichen cover the rock, with stunted pine and sweetgum adding their interesting shapes. The trail again meanders for a short distance then enters a more mature hardwood forest. At 1.1 miles arrive at the unmarked south access to Lost Falls. This side trail leads north for 80' to the top of the falls. (You may continue on the blue trail here or shortcut and intersect the orange trail.)

When seen under the right conditions this 8'-high waterfall and its downstream neighbor, Laurel Falls, are beautiful sights.

After the falls, the blue trail narrows significantly as it meanders and follows a couple of wet-weather streambeds. At 1.35 miles cross a small branch via a footbridge and enter a large area of exposed rock. This is one of the more scenic spots on this hike. Mosses and lichens cover much of the smooth, rippling sandstone found here. Stunted pines and the skeltons of their predecessors add starkness to this beautiful setting. (Trail markings are painted on the bedrock here.)

After crossing the exposed rock, at 1.4 miles intersect the orange trail which leads both right and left. Take the trail on the right and reenter the woods. From this point much of the orange trail treads over exposed sandstone or loose sand. The forest floor here is carpeted in mosses and lichens thriving in the woodland shade. At 1.6 miles arrive at the north access side trail to Lost Falls. There may be a sign here stating "Lost Falls." This trail leads 100' to the top area.

One and three-fourths miles into the hike, cross an exposure of sandstone with a small trickling branch cutting into it. In .2 of a mile, the yellow trail from the campground intersects on the left. At 2.2 miles arrive at a short side trail leading to the top of Laurel Falls.

This waterfall spills 8' over a shelf-like overhang into a tree-lined pool below. Of special note here are euonymus and the huge leaved umbrella magnolia.

Back on the loop, at 2.4 miles cross a small wet-weather branch in another area of exposed rock. Just ahead a pathway branches off to the left leading to the campground. The orange trail bends right then left as it passes by large boulders on the right. At 2.5 miles arrive at intersection "A" (near trail marker #7) on the red-blazed Azalea Cascade Trail. At 2.7 miles arrive at the intersection of the A and B trails. To complete the loop, continue straight ahead and walk among huge sandstone boulders, some the size of a small two-story house. Turn right and pass through Needle Eye Rock before exiting the woods at the Azalea Cascade Trailhead. A right turn leads to the parking area .1 of a mile away.

2. Indian Falls - Lodge Falls

Map: Desoto State Park
Loop .9 of a mile, water crossing, moderate

Directions: See Lost and Laurel Falls.

There is a sign on the west side of the road at this location, with an arrow pointing east, that states "Indian Falls."

Enter the clearing on the *east* side of Hwy. 89 and pass the sewage treatment plant. In 260' bisect the white and yellow trails. (The white trail goes both left and right here, while the yellow-blazed Desoto Scout Trail goes both right and straight ahead.) Indian Falls is 25' straight ahead from this point and its base is reached via a 50' side path.

Ten to 12' high, this waterfall flows over the deep overhang of a rock shelf. A tree beside the falls, when viewed from the south side, has what appears to be

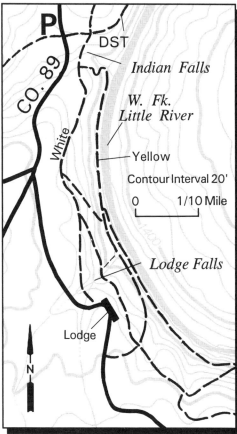

a lightning-split trunk. When I visited the falls, water was pouring over the ledge and streaming down this split—following every curve.

Return to the point where you bisected the trails and hike south on the white- and yellow-blazed trail. You'll immediately cross a footbridge over the top of Indian Falls. At just under .1 of a mile the yellow trail veers left and downhill, while the white trail continues along the cliff edge. (Don't take the unmarked pathway on the extreme right as it leads to cabins.) Take the white trail, you'll soon pass through the backyard of a cabin then reenter the woods. In this vicinity the West Fork of the Little River is visible below. At .2 of a mile an unmarked trail takes off to the left and leads down to connect with the return trail— disregard it. From this point the white trail climbs at a moderate rate over rubble and past some huge boulders. At .3 of a mile a path leads to a cabin on the right. The white trail levels somewhat and in just over 300', forks. Take the left fork which leads to the base of Lodge Falls. (The right fork crosses the fall's branch above the falls then leads to the lodge and restaurant .1 of a mile ahead.) Forty feet from this point pass by a confusing path on the left. The next highlight is some very nice overhanging cliffs on the right side of the trail. These appear to have iron mixed in with the sandstone. I found cardinal flower and euonymus in this area. At .45 of a mile pass by the falls which are 60' off the trail on the right.

With adequate water Lodge Falls is very pretty. The creek's waters cling to this 60'-wide blocky cliff before letting go in a 15' drop. The creek then rushes as cascades down through a cove of moss-covered boulders.

The white trail crosses the creek on steppingstones just below these cascades. (There is a potentially confusing pathway here leading down alongside the creek.) From the crossing the trail climbs and bends right to round the hillside. At the half-mile point, the white trail crosses an unmarked but well-worn trail. (A right turn leads 325' to the parking area just south of the lodge and restaurant.) Turn sharply left here and take this unmarked trail to complete the loop.

The unmarked trail descends at a moderate rate and at .55 of a mile again crosses Lodge Falls Branch. Pass through ankle-deep galax lining the trail and winterberry bushes, which in late summer are loaded with clusters of red berries. Just after crossing this branch, the shortcut pathway from Lodge Falls intersects on the left. At .6 of a mile pass by a shortcut on the right that connects at the river's edge with the yellow trail. Just ahead, pass an unmarked trail on the left which leads uphill to connect with the white trail (mentioned on the way in). At .65 of a mile the unblazed route now joins and treads the yellow trail, which continues upstream after intersecting from the right.

Just ahead, notice a riverside outcrop of rock with a great view both up and downstream. At .8 of a mile pass down then up through a rocky low spot beside the river. (During periods of high water the trail may be partially submerged here.) Approaching Laurel Creek pass by a stretch of scenic rock bluffs on the left. With the creek in sight, the trail turns sharply left and switchbacks up the hill (a slim path here leads straight ahead to Laurel Creek). At .9 of a mile tie back into the white trail near Indian Falls. A right turn leads back to the parking area.

Little River Canyon National Preserve

Note: Heed the warning signs: a fall at any of the overlooks would lead to certain injury or possibly death. Keep in mind that loose sand on top of sandstone is like having hundreds of tiny ball bearings underfoot.

Directions: From the Desoto State Park country store and information center, drive south on County Hwy. 89 for approximately 5.8 miles. Turn left (east) onto Ala. Hwy. 35 and drive 5.35 miles to Ala. Hwy. 176 (Little River Canyon Parkway) on the right. Little River Canyon is accessed via a 22 mile scenic drive (Ala. Hwy. 176 and Co. Rd. 275) that winds along its west rim. Before you take this drive check out Little River Falls (see below).

Alternate Directions: From U.S. Hwy. 11, in Ft. Payne, drive east on Ala. 35 for 7.75 miles to Ala. 176 (Little River Canyon Parkway).

Little River Falls,
Dekalb and Cherokee Counties, Ala.

U.S.G.S. Quadrangle: Ft. Payne, Ala. A "10"   No hiking map needed.
Side view 350', easy, base .4 of a mile, difficult

Note: There are exposed cliffs here so be very careful. If venturing to the base, check to be sure that the east channel of the river is dry.

Directions: From Hwy. 176 continue east on Hwy. 35 (crossing the river bridge) for an additional .25 of a mile. The parking area is on the right.

From the parking area, walk downhill via steps for 100' then take a slim pathway downstream for 250' to a grand side view of this thundering giant.

The base can be reached via the pathway that continues downstream along the rim. Hike an additional .2 of a mile from the side view to a point where the trail appears to dead end. Look carefully for a split in the rock cliff that forms a narrow passageway down into the canyon. At the cliff base descend to river level over a talus-covered slope. Hike or boulder hop upstream along the east channel of the river, or along the base of the cliffs, to the base of the falls.

The might of this waterfall is best captured on a blue-sky day with the sun high overhead. This enables the use of a small aperture for sharpness and a fast, action-stopping shutter speed. Set your tripod up low enough so the highway bridge and its traffic are cropped out of the frame.

Gregg's Two Falls

U.S.G.S. Quadrangle: Little River, Ala., A "6" collectively
.2 of a mile, moderate-difficult

Note: These waterfalls are best seen after adequate winter or spring rains. My first visit here was in the early fall. Being a normally dry time of year, the falls were barely a trickle. Although the falls are small, their setting is among the most picturesque and unusual around. To capture all of the surrounding beauty you need a panorama camera. This location photographs best under the diffused lighting of an overcast day.

Directions: From Ala. Hwy. 35, drive south on Hwy. 176 for 5.2 miles to the pullout on the right. (For further verification, the fall's creek [Wolf Creek] passes under the highway through a culvert which is protected by guardrails on both sides of the road. Also, County Road 255 intersects Hwy. 176 on the right approximately 300' before you arrive at the pullout.) The pathway to the falls begins at the east end of the south guardrail.

As you leave the roadway the path treads through tall grasses then enters the tree line where it closely follows Wolf Creek. After passing over small boulders and skirting a rock overhang, at 380' the pathway becomes harder to discern because of recent windfalls. Visitors taking different routes around them have not made a clearly worn track. If in doubt about which path to take, opt for the one closest to the creek. At 775' pass by the top of the upper falls. In just over 50' look for a slimmer side path that leads via a switchback to creek level.

This waterfall is located in a semi-circular alcove which is 40' wide with a 40' cliff on the left side. The falls spill 10' off the rock shelf and splash onto a boulder that has fallen away from the overhang. After heavy rains the creek covers the full width of the rock shelf and fills the creekbed as well.

To reach the lower falls return to the main pathway and hike downstream for another 300'. Here you'll find a steep pathway descending into the alcove. If the creek level is down considerably, you'll find that even the slightest sounds you emit are echoed back.

The lower falls are very unusual. On my first visit I encountered only a small trickle dropping into a dammed pool. I could walk across this talus dam dryshod, as it was five feet higher than pool level. There was not enough water flow to build the pool up sufficiently to make up for the seepage loss and thus flow over the natural dam. The only outlet for the creek then, was to seep and flow through the talus. Under low-water conditions the creek becomes a mini "lost creek," resurfacing two-hundred feet down the canyon. This blue-green pool is deep and contains small fish. It appears that their passageway is cut off completely until adequate rains refill the pool.

On my next visit, heavy rainfall had changed this totally. The talus dam was now underwater and there was no way to safely cross the raging creek for a better camera position. I came back 24 hours later to a kinder—gentler Wolf Creek and was able to reach the high point of the dam easily.

What makes this waterfall such a beauty is the overhanging semicircular alcove and the symmetry of its cleft sandstone. Oak leaf hydrangea decorates the cracked rock of this strange and scenic place.

Grace's High Falls

This wet-weather waterfall is seen approximately 1000' across Bear Creek Canyon from a pullout along Hwy. 176, .1 of a mile south of the 19 milepost (approximately 7 miles from Hwy. 35).

Dry much of the year, this 125' waterfall is thought to be Alabama's highest.

South Cumberland State Recreation Area

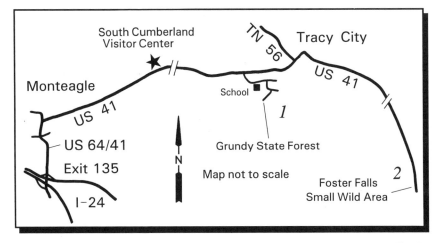

Directions: From Chattanooga or Nashville, take I-24 to exit 135 (the Monteagle exit). Turn north onto U.S. 64/41 and in .6 of a mile turn right onto U.S. 41 South (Fairmont Ave.). There may be a sign here "South Cumberland Visitor Center." Drive 2.5 miles and arrive at the visitor center which is on the left. Stop by for a brief and informative geology and history lesson.

Unless otherwise noted the falls on pgs. 101-112 are located in Grundy County, Tennessee.

From the South Cumberland Visitor Center, take U.S. 41 South to access the following points of interest:

1. Third St., access to Grundy State Forest: 2.3 miles.
2. Foster Falls Small Wild Area: 11.2 miles.

1. Grundy Forest Day Loop, (Hanes Hole, Blue Hole, and Sycamore Falls)

Roads: Paved   Map: Handout at visitor center
Loop trail, white blazed, 1.9 miles, minor water crossings, moderate
Sycamore Falls via Fiery Gizzard Trail adds 1.2 miles round trip.

Directions: As you leave the visitor center, zero your odometer and turn left (south) onto 41 South. Drive 2.3 miles to Third St. and turn right. (When I visited the area, the route was marked with signs reading "Grundy Forest State Natural Area." If the signs are missing look for the Sequatchee Valley Electric Cooperative office on the southeast corner of this intersection, and continue with the following directions.) Pass the Tracy City Elementary School, on the right, and in .4 of a mile turn right again. Pass by the fairgrounds and in .2 of a mile turn sharply right onto a road that runs between the fairgrounds and a residential area. In .1 of a mile pass the Fiery Gizzard Trail overnight and backpacker's parking area, which is on the right. Continue another .1 of a mile, crossing a small intersection while en route to the picnic shelters and day loop trailhead.

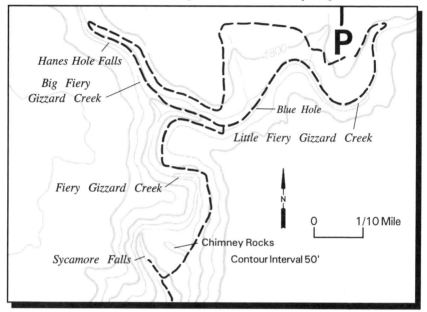

The trail begins to the right of the Pavillion Group Picnic Shelter located at the apex of the parking area. (This is to the right of the C.C.C. monument, seen as you enter the park.) Directions given below are for hiking the loop in a counterclockwise direction.

From the picnic shelter, the trail immediately enters the woods, bends right, and treads upon exposed bedrock, surrounded by patches of haircap moss and lichen. Descending at an easy rate, in 400' cross School Branch on steppingstones just above a small wet-weather waterfall. (This will be explored from its base on the return portion of the loop.) The trail turns right after crossing the creek then leads uphill. Meandering through sparse pines and small hardwoods the trail soon tops out. At .15 of a mile cross a bog on a boardwalk and then enter a more mature forest with intermittent American holly and hemlock. At .3 of a mile, in another bog, cross a footbridge over a small dissipating branch. The trail then turns left and follows the west side of this bog (which regains creek status further down the drainage). The trail now meanders through a hardwood forest and the flat land of the bog gives way to the slopes of a hollow. The trail parallels the reemerging creek, then drifts west and away from the hollow's depths. At .45 of a mile arrive at a sandstone bluff with an 8-10' cliff. Here, the trail turns sharply right. The rushing sound of Little Fiery Gizzard Creek (not associated with eating Mexican food) can be heard below.

At the half-mile point, pass a small but noticeable water-filled depression on the right side of the trail. The trail leads away from the bluffs here for deeper woods. Just ahead, 50' right of the trail, is the rock foundation of a C.C.C. camp. After meandering, the trail bends left and leads close to the bluffs again. The treadway then turns right and parallels the bluffs at a distance as they progressively lessen and become slopes. At two thirds of a mile pass through a thicket of small hardwoods. As you exit them, the rushing Big Fiery Gizzard Creek makes its presence known below on the left. After crossing a wet-weather branch, top a small rise. Here, the trail begins to descend into the Big Fiery Gizzard Gorge and into a more moisture tolerant forest of hemlock with patches of the ground cover partridgeberry dressing its slopes. At .85 of a mile the trail bends sharply left, passes a large boulder on the right, and joins Big Fiery Gizzard Creek, descending in unison with its eastern bank. Seen on the cascading creek's west side are scenic cliffs. The trail is narrowed here by the steepness of the hillside on the left and the creekbank on the right. At just over a mile arrive alongside Hanes Hole Falls and its plunge pool.

The creek slides 70', then leaps off a sandstone shelf that is sheared off diagonally across the creek. Although the falls are only 6' high, the beauty of the blue hole into which they fall and the surrounding moss-covered rocks more than make up for their small size.

In approximately 100' look for a steep access route to the base. Looking downstream from this vantage point, the creek cascades over talus then out of sight in a right bend between the steep hillsides.

Back on the loop trail, from this point to the confluence of Big and Little Fiery Gizzard Creeks, at 1.2 miles, the trail descends steeply over rock and is made one-foot-in-front-of-the-other slim by the steep hillsides. At the confluence, the trail turns upstream along Little Fiery Gizzard Creek and descends a rocky stretch to creek level. At 1.3 miles arrive at the footbridge over Little Fiery Gizzard Creek. This is the trailhead for the Fiery Gizzard Trail and leads to Sycamore Falls. (See directions below.)

Continuing on the loop, pass by the piers of an old bridge. The trail becomes more rugged as it undulates upstream over rocky stretches. Scenic bluffs and big leaf magnolia line the creeksides as it cascades and pools through boulders covered thick in moss. At 1.45 miles arrive at Blue Hole Falls.

The falls are 5' high and flow over the protruding lip of a deep rock shelf, similar to that found at Hanes Hole. Falling into a 35'-wide pool, its greatest depth is 20' out from its splash point. The evergreen colors of hemlock, laurel, and moss-covered rocks accentuate the beauty of its blue-green pool. The best view is 100' or so downstream, where hemlock boughs frame the setting and the shallow foreground waters churn white. A tumbling creek on the left flows over the trail and joins the Blue Hole plunge pool 50' below the falls.

Carefully cross the tributary branch over slick rock and continue upstream. At 1.6 miles cross School Branch on steppingstones. Up its cove a 15' wet-weather waterfall (mentioned at the outset), falls over a beautiful sandstone ledge. An exploratory path leads steeply up its left side for 200' to the base.

Back on the loop trail, round a rocky bend and pass through a low spot that may be under water after heavy rains. Climbing out of the flood plain the trail leaves the creek momentarily and heads for the laurel and a drier microclimate. At 1.85 miles pass under the Cave Spring Rockhouse (a huge sandstone overhang). There are large moss-covered boulders here as well. The trail now turns steeply uphill and becomes very rocky. Soon the trail turns sharply left and zigzags through the rock to the top of the bluff. Atop the rockhouse the trail turns right and heads for the parking area 150' away.

<u>Sycamore Falls:</u> Cross the footbridge in a setting of beautiful rock bluffs. The Fiery Gizzard Trail starts out at stream level treading an old roadbed. In 480' pass the confluence of Big and Little Fiery Gizzard Creeks at the head of Black Canyon (so named for the color of its exposed shale). Notice the multiple layers of shale exposed by the creek's downward cut. An 8' waterfall is formed at the canyon's head by the creek being forced into a rock flume 10-15' wide which then narrows to 5'. Fast, violent, and dangerous, enjoy the sights at a distance. The trail through Black Canyon is very rocky and root laced with several stratified rock overhangs. Just downstream there are several boulders that have fallen away from the rock walls while others await their turn. The moss covering the rock in the creekbed here is made a deeper green by the dark underlying shale.

At the quarter-mile point the trail heads up the rocky hillside, climbing at a moderate rate, to circumvent a bluff. At .35 of a mile, in the midst of a boulder slide, notice a huge boulder downstream with enough mass to have topsoil and trees growing atop it. White blazes guide the way through the slide's rubble then back down to creek level where the Chimney Rocks soon come into view. These are large, stratified sandstone boulders left standing at the base of the ridge line. Big Fiery Gizzard Creek bends sharply right and flows around the Chimney Rocks. The trail climbs, bends slightly left, crosses a small branch, then passes through a gap in the Chimney Rocks. At the half-mile point the trail bends right then meanders downward into the two-tier creek bottom. At .55 of a mile, in an open stand of hemlock, arrive at a Y intersection. The Fiery Gizzard Trail continues left and the blue-blazed Sycamore Falls Trail branches off to the right. A wooden sign announces "Sycamore Falls."

Hike the side trail for 350' to a side view of the falls. A slim pathway near the downstream end of the pool leads steeply down to a large boulder where the falls can be seen in their entirety.

The falls are 10' high with a 50' by 50' blue-green plunge pool. Look for a hornets' nest dangling high above the pool. There's a high, wet-weather waterfall cascading off the cliffs on the west side of Big Fiery Gizzard Creek that enters the drainage just above the falls.

If photographing from the base, the rock overhang on the right side of the pool casts harsh shadows. An off-camera flash is needed to lighten it within the tonal range of films.

2. Foster Falls Small Wild Area

Roads: Paved   An "8" 60'
Map: Handout at visitor center
.2 of a mile, easy   No hiking map needed.

At this location, turn right into the Foster Falls Small Wild Area. In .45 of a mile arrive at the parking area and trailhead. The trail begins at the trail register located on the left (south) side of the parking area (sign: 125 yards to falls).

Enter the woods on this easy trail and in 210' cross a small branch on a footbridge. Exit the woods at 320' and pass under a power line on the clearly-worn pathway. At 450' arrive at a walled viewing area on the canyon's rim.

This overlook provides the most complete view of the falls, however, the lower portion is not visible here. Upstream, in the next 400', are two more overlooks along the rim where the missing pieces may be seen.

In winter, when the falls flow full bore, they are approximately 25' wide. The creek is channeled through a V-shaped gorge, then falls over the rim into a huge amphitheater that has been undercut and carved out over the ages. The left wall is approximately 100' high, while the right wall is 70-80'. Hemlock trees cap the rim and scrub pines cling to the cliffs. The plunge pool is 90' wide and 60' out with a deep, fast flowing creek exiting it. The falls are especially beautiful with a blue sky as a backdrop.

South and Central Cumberland Area Map

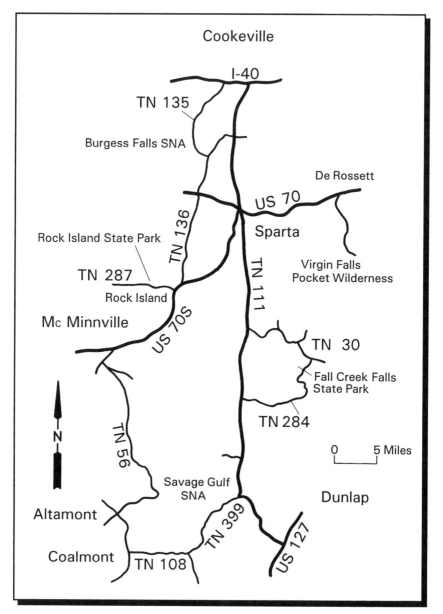

Cookeville

I-40

TN 135

Burgess Falls SNA

De Rossett

US 70

TN 136

Sparta

Rock Island State Park

TN 287

Virgin Falls
Pocket Wilderness

Rock Island

TN 111

Mc Minnville

US 70S

TN 30

Fall Creek Falls
State Park

TN 284

0   5 Miles

N

TN 56

Savage Gulf
SNA

Dunlap

Altamont

TN 399

US 127

Coalmont

TN 108

Note: Individual Area Maps are not provided for the following locations: Fall Creek Falls State Park; Rock Island State Park and; Burgess Falls SNA. Please use this map as an aid in locating them. In addition, other locations with more detailed Area Maps are plotted here as well.

106

Altamont - Coalmont Area

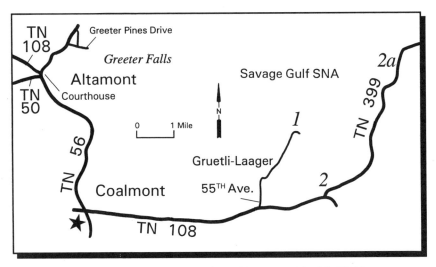

Greeter and Boardtree Falls, Savage Gulf SNA

Roads: Paved   A "10" & "3" respectively
U.S.G.S. Quadrangle: Altamont, Tn.
White blazed, Greeter Falls .6 of a mile, Boardtree Falls .25 of a mile additional.

Directions: From the courthouse in Altamont, drive north on Tn. Hwy. 56 for 1.3 miles to Greeter Pines Drive (sign: "Greeter Falls"). Turn right and in .7 of a mile arrive at the parking area on the left. The trail begins on the right (south) side of the road at an iron gate with a sign stating "Greeter Falls Trail, .5 of a mile to Greeter Falls, Boardtree Falls, 1 mile."

As you enter the woods the trail treads a wide and level roadbed while passing through a predominantly pine forest. At 310' the trail turns left. In another 200' it turns right and begins to descend at an easy to moderate rate. At .2 of a mile arrive at a spot where the road continues left and the trail turns off right. The trail now narrows, descends more steeply, and at the quarter-mile point parallels the east bank of a small wet-weather branch. In 100', the trail bends sharply left while the small branch flows over the cliff. (This is a dangerous area as the trail is protected from the precipice by only a thin row of laurel with Firescald Creek far below.) After passing a sandstone outcrop the trail enters a laurel thicket then turns steeply down towards the base of the bluffs. At .4 of a mile look for a side trail which may be marked by a sign pointing right stating "Upper Falls." As well, there may be a sign pointing left stating "Lower Falls, Boardtree Falls."

Take the Upper Falls side trail which descends and leads upstream. In 175' arrive at a viewing area alongside the falls.

107

The Upper Falls are very pretty, spilling 8′ over a vertical fissure that couldn't have been laid with more precision by a brick mason. This fissure is evident from the viewpoint as it runs diagonally across the 90′ width of the creekbed before disappearing into the woods. There is a large boulder in the middle of its flow then a larger one above the falls with trees growing atop it (an island of sorts). Hundreds of layers of stratified shale are visible here and slippery footing is an ever-present danger atop it. There is no sandstone layer at creek level (as in other locations): it lies on the gulf's rim. Hemlocks flank its sides and alders sprout

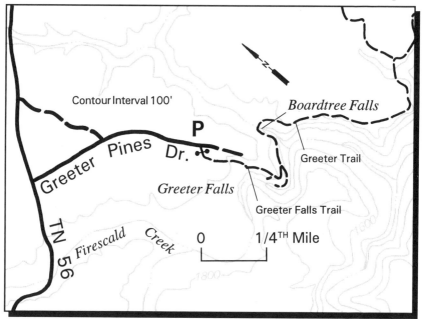

out of the cracked rock. Hardwoods provide the backdrop on distant slopes.

The Greeter Falls Trail continues downstream along the bluff line and at .45 of a mile bends sharply left to connect with the Greeter Trail. At this juncture the Greeter Trail veers left and uphill, while the Greeter Falls Trail turns sharply right and downhill to access the base. (Signs here give directions and distances.)

From this point the Greeter Falls Trail is rocky for approximately 100′ then turns sharply right and descends a better treadway. At 370′, while passing alongside the overhanging shale cliffs, notice a small tunnel straight ahead, and large boulders in Firescald Creek down the steep slope. (Be very careful in this area. In one spot in particular the cliff overhangs the trail at head height: you could lose your balance while leaning to get around it. Underfoot the trail is narrow, sloping, and treads over loose shale chips. To make matters worse, if you lost your footing there is nothing to stop you from sliding into the rocky creek far below.) After climbing then descending in-ground steps the trail enters the amphitheater housing the falls. At 715′ descend a long flight of stairs and a slick ramp to the base of this super beauty.

Housed in a 200'-wide amphitheater, this 50' waterfall plunges with a constant roar into a large, blue-green pool. The shale cliffs on its sides are 60-70' high with flat slabs of sandstone littering the base of the cirque. Mist kicked up by the falls covers the rocks on the downstream end of the plunge pool making them slick with algae. During cold weather these rocks and the lower flight of stairs glaze with ice.

To visit Boardtree Falls return to the Greeter Trail junction.

Boardtree Falls: From the Greeter Falls Trail, the main trail (now known as the Greeter Trail) turns sharply left and ascends towards the sandstone bluff. In 200' the trail turns right and parallels the base of the cliffs, treading over talus. At 400' the trail turns away from the cliffs and downhill over rubble then bottoms out. As the trail turns left, ascending back towards the rock wall, the rushing Boardtree Creek can be heard on the right. The trail undulates over heavy talus bending in unison with the cliffs that now form the cove for Boardtree Creek. Two tenths of a mile from the Greeter Falls Trail arrive at a very noticeable, jutting sandstone overhang. Boardtree Falls is approximately 200' ahead. The best route to its base is near this overhang.

Look for a steep pathway through the talus and ferns to creek level 150' away. The falls are seen upstream 150-200' away.

The steep-banked creek is very scenic. Its rush is broken by small clear pools and medium-size moss and lichen-covered sandstone boulders. The fall's upper tier is 8-10' high, while its lower tier is 20'. Facing southeast, Boardtree Falls is best photographed on an overcast day or in the early morning or late afternoon. Otherwise deep shadows are cast into its cove by the high sun.

Coalmont Area

Directions: From the intersection of Tn. Hwys. 56 and 108 in the community of Coalmont, drive east on Hwy. 108 to the following points of interest. (See Area Map contained within Greeter Falls.)

1. 55TH Ave. (sign: "Gruetli-Laager Recreational Park"), access to Suter and Horsepound Falls (Savage Gulf SNA): 5.35 miles.
2. The intersection of Tn. Hwy. 399: 7.4 miles. Take Tn. 399 the following distance to:
   2(a) Savage Gulf State Natural Area (access to Savage Falls): 5.15 miles.

1. Suter and Horsepound Falls, Savage Gulf SNA

Roads: Paved   A "10" & "6" respectively
U.S.G.S. Quadrangle: Collins, Tn.
White blazed, 2.5 miles, water crossing, moderate, trail closed when iced

Directions: At this location turn left (north) onto 55TH Ave. There is an imitation stone-type concrete block building on the northwest corner of this intersection. En route to trail parking the road's name changes to Swiss Memorial Road. Drive 2.75 miles to a point where the road bends sharply right. As you enter this hard turn, look for the parking area which lies straight ahead. Pull off to the right side of the parking area as this is a bus turnaround.

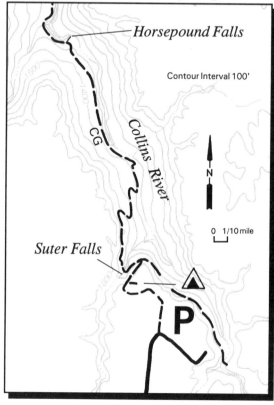

Horsepound Falls

Contour Interval 100'

CG

Collins River

N

0 1/10 mile

Suter Falls

From the parking area, the Collins Gulf Connector Trail heads due north on an old roadbed, descending at an easy rate. At approximately .2 of a mile the trail turns left, immediately crosses a footbridge and enters the woods. The trail turns uphill and soon levels. At .3 of a mile pass the south access to the Collins West Campsite. (A sign here gives directions and distances.) At .4 of a mile arrive at an old roadbed. The trail turns right and treads the road. In 120' pass the west access to the Collins West Campsite.

Continue on the Collins Gulf Connector and descend the steep and rocky trail for another .1 of a mile to connect with the Collins Gulf Trail.

From this juncture hike the Collins Gulf Trail north (left) as it undulates over a jumble of medium-size boulders. The trail then rises and tops the north-sloping ridge line. (Beware of a steep drop-off in this area.) After topping this rise the trail descends its western downslope and while bending left passes under a small icy shower (in the wet season). Here, the sweeping half-circle rock overhang preceding the falls comes into view. As you enter the alcove (.55 of a mile), Rocky Mountain Creek comes into view far below as a 10-12' stairstep cascade. The trail passes under the overhang where the ceiling and the floor (created from its talus) meet in clamshell fashion. The overhang progressively deepens and along with the creek continues bending right. At .6 of a mile Suter Falls comes into full view approximately 250' away.

This is one of the better spots to view and photograph them. Choose an overcast day to avoid harsh lighting. The falls are veiled by hemlock and framed in a most becoming way by the overhang, which is now 40' high. The stark beauty of the overhang is balanced out by the delicacy of the falls. Suter Falls fans out as it free falls 30' from a cliff at the far end of the rock shelf. Moss-covered rocks dot the creekbed preceding the base. The bluff to its right is rugged and very scenic.

Approximately 150' downstream from the falls the trail turns right and descends precariously over unstable talus to creek level. (A side trail continues under the diminishing overhang towards the falls.) The trail is hard to make out in the talus, but if you'll look for it on the far side of the creek and project it back towards you, the best route is easily seen. The creek is easily hopped and at stream level you may see the white blazes marking the route.

On the north side of the creek, large boulders offer some of the better close-up views of what is surely one of the most unusual spots in the East.

Continuing, pick up the white blazes on the north side of the creek and head through a maze of boulders and rhododendron. A keen eye is needed here to stay on track. Generally, the trail passes straight across the creek and into the boulders, then turns left and climbs to intersect the bluff from which the falls plunge. At the base of the bluff turn right and tread over heavy talus that teeters underfoot. The talus lightens up somewhat for a short distance then gets heavier as you approach then cross a small creek. At .85 of a mile, in winter, when looking southeast, the bluffs near the Collins West Campsite and those of the Collins Gulf can be seen.

At .9 of a mile the trail makes a pass between the bluffs and a rocky high point of conglomerate sandstone boulders. The browns, grays, golds, and greens of the bluff walls found here are especially scenic when set against a blue sky. Northbound while exiting this pass, the trail becomes much easier as it treads over less rubble. At 1.1 miles reach a right turn (the first of three switchbacks). The trail meanders through a forest of hickory, oak, and poplar as it descends towards the Collins River. At 1.45 miles the trail turns left to follow the river downstream. Notable at 1.5 miles are mossy boulders on both sides of the trail.

Descending the third switchback, the trail lands on an old roadbed with the beautiful blue-green Collins River flowing 100' away. Now undulating, the trail is much easier in the river bottom (easy-moderate), although there are some wet spots. Boulders and fallen logs in the river's moist environ are dripping green with moss.

At 1.95 miles, the trail turns downhill slightly, leaves the roadbed and undulates through a stand of small sycamore trees, then rejoins the road. At 2.35 miles the trail exits a small S, straightens up for a short distance, then bends left and descends. Seen through the trees in winter are bluffs to the northwest. In this bend (2.45 miles) lies the side trail to Horsepound Falls.

Take the steep side trail for 370' down to the top of the falls. Near the top, look to the left for a slim pathway leading down among the huge boulders at the base for a better view. This 15'-high, 25'-wide waterfall falls over a stratified limestone ledge into a clear-green plunge pool. A steep-sloping mountain provides a backdrop to them. The Collins River, deep and swift, is narrowed to 10' between bedrock on the pool's south side and the island-like build-up of tumbled river rock on its north side. White and gray limestones form the ledge from which the falls plunge. The uppermost layer of limestone is almost 2' thick and its base is 12' higher than pool level. Downstream the Collins River makes a sharp S and disappears from view.

Initially, I was not overly impressed with Horsepound Falls. Its beauty is just above average. But the more I investigated, the more amazed I became with this living part of the earth. At work here are the dynamics that shape our planet.

While at the base, peer under the upper limestone ledge. Notice that driftwood has been deposited on the shelves of its deep recesses. On the north side of the plunge pool notice the huge 12'-high pile of river rock. I was told by the rangers that in December of '91 more than 10" of rain fell on the area in a short period. The slide behind the falls (on the west-facing slope) is a result of that great rain which undermined and moved boulders and eventually lead to the earth above coming down. The driftwood under these ledges, the rock pile and the like, are the remnants of that, or similar floods over the ages. It's hard to imagine that kind of natural violence here.

2. The intersection of Tn. Hwy. 399 (as above).

2(a) Savage Falls, Savage Gulf SNA

Roads: Paved   An "8"
U.S.G.S. Quadrangle: Collins, Tn.
White blazed, 1.55 miles, minor water crossings, easy

Directions: Turn left into the park's entrance and drive .1 of a mile to the parking area. A walkway on the right leads to the ranger station and trail access. The Savage Day Loop (trail to the falls) begins at the information board on the right side of the ranger station. Distances to other objectives are given here as well.

Level at the outset, the trail passes through a mixture of pine and hardwoods with an open field to the left. At 485' a blue-blazed side trail leads left to a campground. The trail descends at an easy rate and at .15 of a mile crosses a footbridge over a wet-weather branch in a wide, low-lying area. In this wetland the forest becomes more diverse adding holly, hemlock, and laurel to its list of credits. The trail winds for the next .15 of a mile then crosses another wet-weather branch over a boardwalk-type footbridge. Leaving a rooty stretch, enter a canopy of laurel then at .35 of a mile cross Boyd Branch on a suspension footbridge. Once across, the trail exits the laurel and leads uphill into a drier microclimate. The trail winds through the hardwoods with haircap moss and partridgeberry lining portions of the treadway. Reach a high point at .65 of a mile; the trail is level for the most part for the next .4 of a mile. At just over 1 mile double white

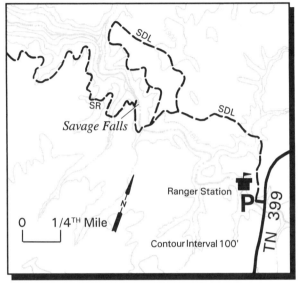

blazes herald the split of the Savage Day Loop. Signs here give trail distances and directions.

Take the left fork and in 200' cross a small branch on a wooden footbridge. One and one-fourth miles into the hike, take the South Rim Trail which leads straight ahead, while the Savage Day Loop goes right. A sign here states "Savage Falls .3 of a mile." At 1.3 miles the South Rim Trail descends a small flight of steps then crosses Savage Creek on a suspension bridge. A beautiful tumbling tributary greets you as you light on the west bank. (Blue blazes mark the trail to the Savage Falls Campsite which is straight ahead here.) The Savage Falls/South Rim Trail leads right and downstream. From the footbridge, the trail ascends through a laurel thicket then tops out at 1.4 miles. The distant falls can be heard from this high point as the trail begins a gradual descent. At 1.45 miles pass the site of a former creekside moonshine still. The creek flows deep here and has a certain calmness about it as well.

At 1.5 miles arrive at the top of the falls. There is a large flat boulder from which to view the plunge pool and its rustic canyon. Be mindful to keep your distance from the dangerous edge!

Just ahead the South Rim Trail bends left (directional signs point left for the Savage Falls Campsite and South Rim Trail). The base trail bisects this bend and leads straight ahead. Descend this side trail via steps into the boulder-strewn plunge-pool area. At 1.55 miles arrive at a point where the beautiful falls are viewed.

Savage Falls has a huge cirque with pine, hemlock, and laurel on its rim. The falls are 15' wide and 20' high and have a thundering rumble about them in full flow. Around the large plunge pool yellow birch is interspersed among conglomerate sandstone boulders. Looking downstream, the cove is filled with a jumble of boulders with the creek crashing violently through them.

For an overall view, return to the intersection of the South Rim Trail and the Savage Day Loop. Hike downstream on the Savage Day Loop which initially leads uphill. In .3 of a mile, after topping out then outlining a couple of small hollows, look for the side trail on the left leading 250' to the overlook. This location may be marked by a sign stating "Dead end trail only. No access into Gorge."

Framed by hemlock, the falls are perhaps 600' away. This overlook is unprotected, so enjoy the sights from a distance!

Fall Creek Falls State Park

Directions: (See Area Map pg. 106). From U.S. 70 in Sparta, drive south on Tn. Hwy. 111 for approximately 23 miles to Tn. Hwy. 284. Drive east on 284

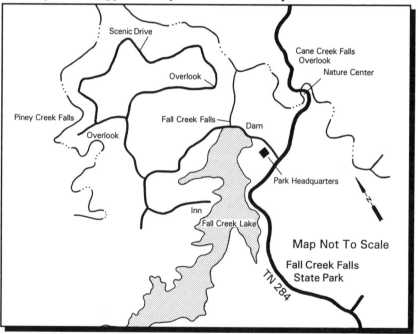

for 10.3 miles to the park's entrance. Follow the park's well-marked routes to the points of interest contained in the text below.

The park's falls lie within Van Buren County, Tennessee.

Fall Creek Falls

Map: Fall Creek Falls State Park,   A "10" 256'
Overlook: 400', very easy; Base: orange blazed, .45 of a mile, moderate

At 256' Fall Creek Falls has the distinction of being the highest free-falling waterfall in the East. Experience the immensity of the falls and its amphitheater with a visit to the base.

The level paved trail to the Fall Creek Falls Overlook begins under a wooden structure with a sign "Foot traffic only, no bicycles."

After walking 400' arrive at the overlook on the right.

The falls are in a deep, bowl-shaped amphitheater that is open to the north with points of land forming two thirds of a circle. Across the gorge, the Rocky

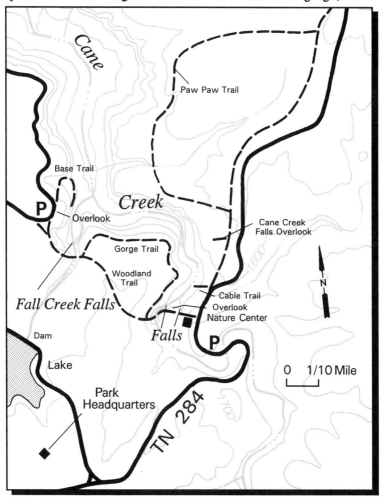

Point Overlook is seen facing north and west, with the Fall Creek Overlook being the other point and east facing. When running fully, the falls are 30' wide at the top and fall 25', pause for a split second, then make an unbroken surging plunge. To the right, Coon Creek makes a more wind-swept, gossamer-like fall. Together they put out a muffled roar and fill the air with mist. During my winter visit the mist drifted like an aimless cloud, sometimes rising as high as the overlook.

Base Trail: The trail to the base begins to the left of the main overlooks. (The connector trail to the Gorge Overlook and Woodland Trails begins on the right. See text pgs. 118-120.) Three-hundred feet from the overlook arrive at a less visited vantage point with a beautiful, albeit veiled view of the falls. (The lower portion of Fall Creek Falls is blocked from view and Coon Creek is completely obscured here.) There is, however, an open view of the Cane Creek and Fall Creek gorges.

The Base Trail is timber lined and graveled part of the way, then descends rock steps. At .2 of a mile pass rock outcrops on the left as the trail makes a sharp bend right. The gnarled roots of hemlocks growing in the cracked rock add their interesting shapes. The trail now descends over rocks, steps, and talus as it switchbacks into the gorge. The talus in this vicinity is covered in light-green lichens. The cliffs become more dramatic and intriguing as you progress downward. Several large sandstone blocks have split away from the walls and slumped towards Fall Creek. One block has a 6' gap between it and where it was previously joined. Through this crevasse another fissured sandstone block is visible that will one day list in the same way. These large blocks are beautifully colored by mosses and lichens.

The trail bends left and parallels the wall of the aforementioned sandstone block before meandering through the talus below. A right turn rounds the sandstone block and the trail now passes under overhanging rock as it enters the fall's alcove. As the ceiling of the overhang increases in height (to 70', with a recess 40' deep) the trail passes through even larger talus. Top a rise at .4 of a mile. This is a good dry spot for photos, with the falls framed by trees. If you care to venture closer, descend the narrow trail along the rock wall. Bear in mind, you're in for a drenching. At .45 of a mile, note the vein of shale underlying the harder sandstone caprock. Because of all of the mist, and not wanting to frizz my doo, I stopped here.

Piney Creek Falls

Map: Fall Creek Falls State Park   A "10" 85'
Orange blazed, 300', easy-moderate   No hiking map needed.

Note: In winter, watch for ice at the overlook.

This trail leads 300', down a rocky treadway, to a flat bedrock viewpoint.

Piney Creek Falls is set in a most beautiful and rugged gorge that seems more typical of the Western States. Mustard-colored lichens adorn its sandstones of gray and rusty brown. Piney Creek has cut deeply into the caprock; the top of the falls are now some 40' lower than the canyon rim. Seen approximately 500' across the gorge, and aptly named for its piney setting, the creek first comes into view on silvery steps. After making a 40' plunge onto the rock below, the waterfall fans out then cascades the rest of its 85'. The mountainous backdrop of pine and hardwoods with wind-bent scrub pine on the rim, makes this the most scenic of the park's waterfalls.

In the wintertime the majority of this waterfall can be seen. In summer, foliage blocks the lower cascades (half of the falls) from view. When photographing with long exposures, watch the foreground hemlocks whose tips move with the slightest wisp of a breeze.

Piney Falls Suspension Bridge: If you haven't experienced a cable-type suspension footbridge, here's the perfect chance. The Piney Falls Suspension Bridge is easily reached and has excellent views to boot.

From the Piney Creek Fall's parking area, hike this descending timber-lined trail. In 330' the graveled treadway gives way to rock and bedrock. At 410' descend rock steps and pass through a laurel thicket. The trail levels out through a rocky stretch and at 625' arrives at the bridge. This bridge sways 35' above beautiful Piney Creek and leads to the western slopes 200' across the way.

I like the suspension bridges of the Cumberland Plateau's parks and hope others will adopt them. I especially like this lofty bridge with its great views of the creek and its rocky cliffs.

Cane Creek Falls

See text for distances. An "8"   See Fall Creek Falls for hiking map.

From the Betty Dunn Nature Center parking area, the Cane Creek Falls Overlook is reached via a 270' paved pathway to the right of the nature center.

The fall's alcove is half-circle shaped and approximately 500' across at its extreme ends. Its cliffs are 100 to 200' high. A smaller (in volume) but higher (125') waterfall on Rockhouse Creek shoots out of the laurel on the right side of the amphitheater. Cane Creek Falls is the park's largest, both in terms of water volume and plunge pool size. At 86', it is the second highest of the park's three major falls.

Cable and Cane Creek Overlook Trails: The orange-blazed Paw Paw Trail begins at the nature center parking area on the access road's north side. The Cable and Cane Creek Overlook Trails spur off this trail. Signs at the trailhead give directions and distances. (White blazes seen here are for the Cane Creek Overnight Trail which shares this treadway.)

The Paw Paw Trail descends steeply over rock and roots and in 100' takes in an open view of Rockhouse Creek. At approximately 200' pass through some tornado damage and then into a rhododendron thicket. At .1 of a mile the trail joins Rockhouse Creek, soon crossing it on steppingstones. (If the creek is up, look carefully for traffic and use the highway bridge to cross on.) One hundred fifty feet from the creek crossing the blue-blazed Cable Trail takes off 90° to the left. (See directions below.) The Paw Paw/Cane Creek Overlook Trail continues straight ahead paralleling the road before reentering the woods.

Now ascending a rocky stretch at a moderate rate, at the quarter-mile point the trail levels off in a forest of hardwoods, pine, and hemlock. Soon thereafter arrive at the trail split. (The Paw Paw Trail continues straight ahead.) Take the Cane Creek Overlook Trail on the left and in 250', after descending moderately, arrive at the fall's viewing area.

This distant vantage point offers a very limited view of the falls, in fact, Cane Creek's plunge pool and Rockhouse Falls are not visible at all.

Cable Trail: This is *the* one trail that I don't have a measured distance on. It's too steep and rough. I estimate it to be 600' in length.

Note: Avoid this trail under icy or otherwise slick conditions. Have your hands free and be unencumbered of packs and camera bags.

A sign at the trail intersection states "Cable Trail, foot of falls" and points the way up the rocky incline. This blue-blazed trail takes a slim route through the laurel. At 140' arrive at a warning sign "Caution hold to the cable. Do not dislodge rocks that may hurt others below. This is a rough climb, if your health is impaired, <u>Do Not Attempt</u>!" At 200' arrive at the cable and the steep, rock trail of sorts, leading to the base.

The trail descends a cliff of rocky steps very steeply into the gorge. Halfway down the cliff-like trail, the taughtness of the cable has it suspended high overhead in an especially tricky spot: the rocky steps are high and steep here and just when you're in need of a handhold, there may not be one.

The trail exits the rhododendron at the downstream end of the plunge pool and onto a rocky beach in the presence of a deep and fast-flowing Cane Creek. Mist from the falls hangs in the air and sometimes drifts as far as the beach, making the rocks slick with algae.

To photograph Cane Creek and its neighbor Rockhouse Falls you must walk towards the plunge pool to obtain a clear shot. I like the view further downstream. This angle singles out Cane Creek Falls and adds interesting rocks to the foreground, leading the eye into the scene.

Gorge Overlook Trail

1.15 miles, easy-moderate   See Fall Creek Falls for hiking map.

From the Betty Dunn Nature Center parking area, round the backside of the center and in 410' cross the suspension bridge just above the Cane Creek cascades. On the creek's west side (600') the trail climbs steps and switchbacks up the slope. After topping the steps, at .15 of a mile, the trail is intersected from the left by the blue-blazed Campground Trail. The Gorge Overlook Trail continues steeply uphill. At the quarter-mile point the yellow-blazed Woodland Trail intersects from the left. (This will serve as the return trail. Signs here give directions and distances.) The Gorge Overlook Trail is red-blazed and also carries the white blaze of the Cane Creek Overnight Trail. The Gorge Overlook Trail reaches a high spot then levels. At .3 of a mile the Gorge Overlook Trail descends progressively steeper then levels out and bends right. Four tenths of a mile into the hike arrive at the side trail for the Cane Creek Overlook. This leads 220' to its namesake.

From this rim-top perch Rockhouse Falls can be fully viewed 500' across the plunge pool, while only the upper half of Cane Creek Falls can be seen.

Back on the Gorge Overlook Trail, the route now undulates, passing through hemlock interspersed with hardwoods. At the half-mile point, bluffs on the east side of the gorge can be seen through the trees. A slim path leads 25' to a boulder on the rim offering a better view. At .65 of a mile, in a level spot of woods, arrive at the Cane Creek Gulf Overlook side trail. This leads 170' to a point where the cliffs on the east rim can be partially seen through the trees. This is a dangerous overlook, so be careful!

The Gorge Overlook Trail is fairly level on the .15 of a mile stretch between the Cane Creek Gulf Overlook and the side trail to the Rocky Point Overlook. This side trail leads 250' to a vantage point atop a jumble of sandstone boulders topped with beautiful wind-swept scrub pine. Be very careful working your way down then up through the boulders to the overlook from which a glimpse of the upper portion of both Fall Creek and its alcove-sharing neighbor, Coon Creek Falls are seen. There are great views of the Cane Creek Gulf and the confluence of Cane and Fall Creeks far below. Seen across the Fall Creek Gulf from this vantage point is the Fall Creek Falls Overlook.

Return to the main trail and in 50' reach the side trail to the Fall Creek Gulf Overlook. This leads 325' down to a rock slab viewpoint 70' east of the falls. Only the fall's upper reaches can be seen here through the treetops.

From the Fall Creek Gulf Overlook side trail the Gorge Overlook Trail descends and in 295' (.85 of a mile into the hike) crosses a small branch then rises slightly. The falls can be heard on the right through the rhododendron. At the top of the rise is a large bedrock exposure. One tenth of a mile from the Fall Creek Gulf Overlook side trail the Woodland Trail intersects on the left. Use this as a return route (see below). (A directional sign points out the routes and gives distances as well.) Continuing towards the Fall Creek Falls Overlook, the trail descends and soon crosses a low wooden bridge over Fall Creek. Now ascending through a canopy of rhododendron, at the 1 mile point the trail tops out then descends again. After crossing the footbridge over Coon Creek arrive at an overlook at 1.1 miles where the Rocky Point Overlook and the upper third of Fall Creek Falls are seen. A pathway nearby splits left and leads to the Fall Creek Fall's parking area. Continue right and tie into the paved Fall Creek Falls Overlook Trail near the restrooms.

Woodland Trail: Return to the yellow-blazed Woodland Trail. This trail makes a right turn off the Gorge Overlook Trail and is an easy to moderate hike winding through a hardwood forest among the rolling hills. Three tenths of a mile from its inception, tie back into the Gorge Overlook Trail to complete the loop.

Rock Island State Park, White and Warren Counties, Tennessee

Roads: Graveled   See Area Map pg. 106.
U.S.G.S. Quadrangles: Doyle, Campaign, Tn.
Very easy

Directions: From U.S. 70S and Tn. Hwy. 287, in the community of Rock Island, take Hwy. 287 (Great Falls Road) for 1.3 miles to the parking area for Great Falls and picnic area #1, on the right. Of special note is the circa 1890 textile mill located here. (The park's headquarters are another mile ahead.)

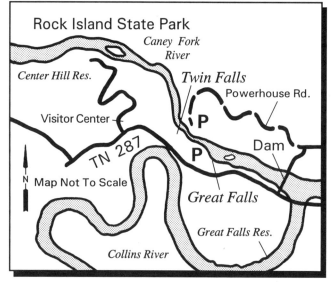

The overlook of Great Falls is at the northeast corner of the parking lot (next to the mill). During my visit the dam's flood gates were closed and the falls were just barely a trickle. There is another overlook at the far end of the parking lot where the more spectacular Twin Falls is seen in the distance as it joins the Caney Fork River downstream.

To visit Twin Falls, return to the Great Falls Dam (passed on the way in, .3 of a mile from the picnic area) and cross the one-lane bridge atop it. This is also known as Great Falls Road (but shown on a county map as being River Road). This road changes to a graveled surface and in .5 of a mile intersects Powerhouse Road. There, turn left and travel another 1.45 miles to the parking area.

120

Walk a slim pathway down to the river's edge and view the falls across the river. Underfoot, imbedded in the limestone are the fossils of ancient corals and vertebrate sea creatures.

Twin Falls is an 80'-high, 200'-wide waterfall that shoots out of the mouths of caves. Its white waters cascade down the mountainside spilling into the Caney Fork River. Now I'm not trying to be an alarmist, but it appears to me to be shooting out the side of the mountain! I was told that the falls erupted when the Great Falls Reservoir was impounded. What started out as two waterfalls is evolving into one. A sort of Siamese Twin Falls with a half-dozen siblings spurting out the hillside as you pan downstream.

The falls are just downstream from, but share the same hillside with the Great Falls Powerhouse.

Burgess Falls State Natural Area, Putnam and White Counties, Tennessee

Roads: Paved   A "10" 130'   See Area Map pg. 106.
U.S.G.S. Quadrangle: Burgess Falls, Tn., Open 8 am to 1/2 hour before dusk.
.55 of a mile to overlook, easy-moderate; Ridge Top Trail .4 of a mile, easy

Directions: From the intersection of U.S. 70 and Tn. Hwy. 111 in Sparta, drive north on 111 for approximately 8.6 miles to the Hwy. 136 South exit. Turn left onto 136 South. After traveling .6 of a mile 136 bends left, retaining its route designation, while taking on the name "Old Kentucky Road North." At 4.3 miles arrive at Bakers Crossroads (4-way stop signs). Turn right onto Burgess Falls Road (Hwy. 135) and drive 3.35 miles to a left turn which leads .2 of a mile (passing the park's headquarters) to the parking area on the left. The River Trail begins at the northwest corner of the parking lot between the picnic area and restrooms.

Alternate directions: From Cookeville, drive south on Tn. Hwy. 135 for approximately 9 miles. After crossing Burgess Falls Lake, take the first right. Drive .2 of a mile to the parking area on the left.

Burgess Falls is named for Tom Burgess who in 1793 was granted land in the area in payment for services rendered during the Revolutionary War. At times the Falling Water River has powered a grist mill, a saw mill, and in the first half of this century two power plants. The first dam and generating plant was lost to a flood in 1928. The dam we now see soon took its place. Made obsolete when larger T.V.A. dams were brought on line, it was taken out of service in 1944.

River Trail: From the parking area, the timber-lined, graveled trail heads towards the river then at 95' turns left and leads downstream. The cascades above the Upper Falls are immediately seen. Crosstie steps lead down to the edge of the beautiful Falling Water River for a closer view. Hiking downstream, at 150' pass by concrete and stone pillars that once held the flume that carried water to a power plant downstream. The trail passes a mossy rock outcrop and the cascading Upper Falls at 375'. An interesting old bridge that once suspended the power plant's flume over the river is located here as well. Across the river note a small tunnel where the pipe entered the rock wall. (Please!, no climbing on the bridge or attempts at spelunking.) The trail passes between two large concrete piers here, bends sharply left, crosses a boardwalk, then passes under rock overhangs.

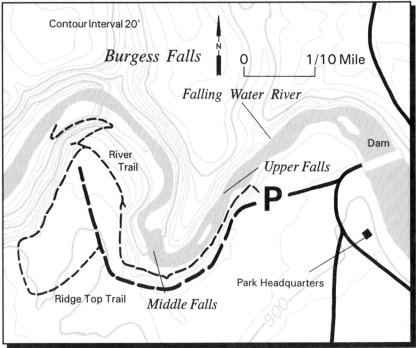

For a short distance the trail remains level while the river continues its drop. At .15 of a mile the trail descends steps and passes a small midstream island. A glance across the river offers views of beautiful, stratified limestone. After crossing a footbridge over a trickling branch with a becoming rock shelf, the trail undulates then bends left and crosses another footbridge at the quarter-mile point. A small shelf-type wet-weather waterfall is seen on the left here.

The top of the Middle Falls come into view as the river and trail bend sharply right. The river disappears over the cliff in a misty and muffled roar. The high bluffs of the Middle Falls Overlook are seen over the top of the falls. The trail tops out at .3 of a mile then descends into the hollow of a wet-weather branch which is crossed on a footbridge. Turning immediately and steeply uphill, in-ground steps lead 200' to surmount the bluff. The Middle Falls are now seen far below on the right. Notice the beautiful bluffs with their muted blacks, browns, and grays and the ever increasing view of the falls. At .4 of a mile, reach the side trail on the right that leads 30' to an observation area above and in front of the Middle Falls.

The Middle Falls are a scenic stairstep-type cascade with a slide on the left. Located in a wide and open area, in full flow they cover 150' of the river's rocky bed (approximately 4/5^{THS} of its width). There is a small midstream island below them. Hemlocks veil the overlook and giant beech trees stand among the laurel and hemlocks on the inland ground.

From the Middle Falls Overlook, the River Trail bends left and descends at an easy rate. At .55 of a mile arrive at the Burgess Fall's observation deck and the side trail to the base. Eighty feet prior to reaching the observation deck is the Ridge Top Trail. (See Ridge Top Trail below.)

Burgess Falls is a powerful, white-water beauty seen from a lofty observation deck on the gorge rim. The Falling Water River has carved a deep chasm over the centuries, with 250' bluffs as its walls. Upstream the bluffs are much lower and topped off by hardwood-covered mountainsides dotted with cedars. Panning the scene from right to left, the barren limestone cliffs to the north become more distant, increasing from 300 to 700' away. You may witness buzzards soaring on thermals high above the river, or returning to their cliff-top roosts.

Base Trail: The trail to the base begins just a few feet east of the observation deck.

Descending in switchback fashion, in .1 of a mile reach river level and the top of the falls. Clamshells litter the river's bedrock where raccoons have feasted. There is a caged stairway (to protect against rockfall) here leading steeply down alongside the thundering falls. As you descend the Base Trail, notice the exposed shale below the limestone layers on the cliff walls to the north.

At the bottom of the steps, a rocky path leads through the mist-filled air to the base of the falls and the upper extremes of Center Hill Lake. Having already had my daily shower, I ended my trip .2 of a mile from the observation deck.

The falls are composed of hundreds of small cascades that when combined form a 130' white-water beauty with deep-green aquatic growth on its sides and in its recesses.

I visited the falls in the winter and feel that spring and summer greenery, or fall colors would liven up the muted colors of the rock found here. In the dry seasons of summer and fall, call ahead to find out about water levels.

Ridge Top Trail: The Ridge Top Trail leads up steps and in 120' levels off as it crosses a service road. Reentering the woods near a prominent cedar tree, the treadway is now graveled and timber lined for a short distance. This portion of the trail outlines the south bluff and provides through-the-trees views of the bluffs to the north. (The falls are no longer seen.) At .1 of a mile, the trail bends sharply left and heads for deeper woods. No longer timber lined, the trail meanders through a forest of beech, maple, oak, poplar, and small hemlock.

The trail then gradually bends left, and on this higher ground is now lined with ferns. At .3 of a mile the trail tops out then descends to the service road. Turn left and hike the road to the beginning point .1 of a mile ahead (.4 of a mile total).

De Rossett Area

Virgin Falls Pocket Wilderness, White County, Tennessee

Roads: Graveled   A "10"
U.S.G.S. Quadrangle: Lonewood, Tn.
8.75 miles round trip, side trails add .7 of a mile, 6-8 hours round trip,
water crossings, moderate-difficult

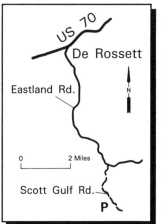

Directions: From Tn. Hwy. 111 and U.S. 70 in Sparta, drive east on U.S. 70 for approximately 11 miles to the community of De Rossett. Turn right (south) onto Eastland Road (shown on local maps as Mulberry Road) and drive 5.85 miles to Scott Gulf Road (sign at the northwest corner of this intersection, "Chestnut Wilderness Forest, Virgin Falls Pocket Wilderness"). Turn right and drive 2.1 miles to the parking area on the right. The trail begins on the north side of the parking area.

Enter the woods and in 200' sign up at the trail register. A sign nearby displays the trail blazes. A green aluminum disc with the stickman hiker symbol denotes the Main Trail. A similar blue disc is the blaze for all side trails.

The trail undulates down then up in the first .2 of a mile, then bends sharply left. Descending into a small hollow, the trail bends left again and crosses a small branch. (This branch rises from the pine thicket bordering the north corridor of the wilderness area. Witness its transition from trickling infancy, to mature-flowing stream.) At .25 of a mile cross the small branch and the trail bends left to meander down its hollow. The first part of the hike is through small hardwoods and pines with an occasional shot of mountain laurel. Trail and creek soon bend sharply right and ply the woods together. At the half-mile point the trail bends sharply left and crosses to the south side of the creek on steppingstones. Once across, the trail turns right and again parallels the creek. For the next .8 of a mile the trail closely follows this small creek in its wide bottom. One of the highlights here is how the creek oxbows like a lazy river. The woodland is gradually giving way to more moisture tolerant plants. American holly, hemlock, and laurel are

124

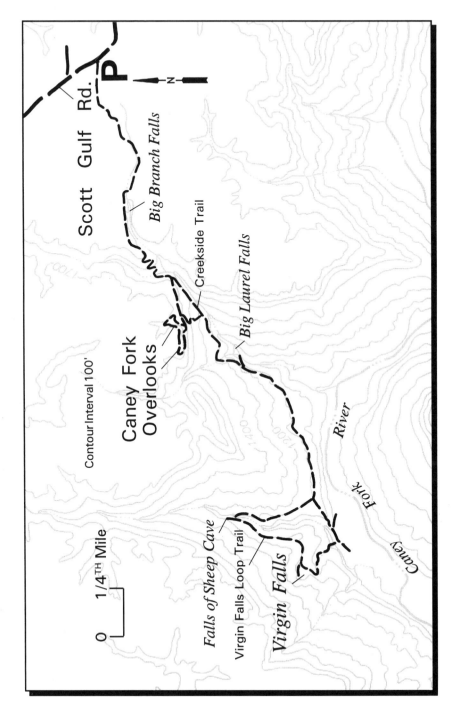

on the increase, as is the volume of water in the creek. At 1.3 miles cross to the creek's north side on table-size steppingstones.

Look for a large mossy rock in the creek at 1.35 miles with a small waterfall sliding over it. This precedes Big Branch Falls whose base is reached via a side trail just over 100' ahead.

Fifty feet off the Main Trail, this 8' cascading waterfall lies in the deep shade with a rockhouse-type overhang on its right side.

From the falls, the trail leaves sight of the creek; its sounds, however, filter through the trees. The next landmark is a large boulder at 1.45 miles. The trail turns sharply left here and switchbacks down the hillside to cross Big Laurel Creek. Once on the west bank, hike downstream on a rocky and root-laced stretch (a preview of the rocks to come). The creek is very colorful, with multiple shades of brown sandstone in coke-bottle green pools. In .1 of a mile the Main Trail turns uphill and slightly away from the creek then splits right at its juncture with what I call the "Creekside Trail." Continue right, we'll use the Creekside Trail (on the left) on our return.

The Main Trail leaves the creek here and makes a bow to the north and west to provide access to the Caney Fork Overlooks. One and seven-tenths miles into the hike (.15 of a mile from the trail junction), after having ascended, arrive at an old roadbed and ascend some in-ground steps. A sandstone bluff becomes visible on the right. Just ahead, the trail levels and parallels the bluffs. Outlining the hollows below these bluffs, with the creek far below, the trail appears to dead end at a large, 30'-long boulder that is angled 45° out of the ground. In this area the trail is sometimes hard to locate among all the rock. The trail crosses a rocky cove and water can be heard, but not seen (unless there has been recent rainfall), as it trickles beneath the rock. For the next 300' or so, the trail meanders through large talus-like boulders then at 1.95 miles arrives at the Caney Fork Overlooks Loop Trail. The largest of these boulders lie where the loop trail takes off from the Main Trail.

Caney Fork Overlooks Loop Trail: With a right turn leave the Main Trail. In 125' the loop trail climbs steps and veers right as it approaches the base of the bluff. Nearing the trickling branch (encountered on the Main Trail), the blue-blazed loop trail climbs a caged ladder then crosses the branch twice as it leads to the first scenic overlook (.2 of a mile off the Main Trail). In another .1 of a mile arrive at the second overlook on a rocky point where stunted and weirdly twisted scrub pine decorate the rock. Both of these overlooks are approximately 50' off the loop. The caged ladder that is used to complete the loop can be seen below and to the right from the second overlook. If it appears too high and steep for you, backtrack out.

Leaving the second overlook, the loop trail descends the second mentioned ladder then switchbacks and descends further to tie back into the Main Trail to complete the .4 of a mile loop.

Main Trail: Back on the Main Trail descend steeply on steps and scattered rubble. Again, the trail is not easily followed as it bends back and forth. There is neither topsoil or fallen leaves among the rock to show a clear track. Keep your eyes open for the green aluminum discs and the intermittent in-ground steps then tie into the west end of the Creekside Trail at 2.1 miles.

Heading downstream through the boulders, the trail turns sharply left and heads towards the creek, then bends right to parallel it. The trail straightens at 2.3 miles as it passes under sandstone bluffs. The creek is 30' below trail level here and sports blue-green pools between the small cascades. The bluffs give way to steep slopes and the creek's rush is hastened. At 2.4 miles arrive alongside Big Laurel Falls. The trail negotiates a tricky boulder-strewn cove and hillside then descends the rocky treadway through a wash of sorts, and winds up in the dry creekbed below the falls. A side trail leads 200' to the base of the falls.

Very scenic, with an amphitheater that is typical of the Cumberland Plateau, a closer look yields its amazing, unique traits. Big Laurel Falls spills 20' over a sweeping, elipse-shaped rock shelf that's perhaps 100' across. The cove downstream is littered with large, moss-covered boulders. Facing the falls and panning left, the wall of the recess behind them increases in depth from 10 to 40'. The falls are 20' wide and flow over the right side of the shelf then disappear into the earth: swallowed into a sinkhole.

Leaving the falls, the trail climbs out of the depths of the dry streambed and treads the somewhat rocky midpoint of the mountainside, with bluffs seen high above. In .2 of a mile the trail bends right to outline the mountainside and its hollows. The trail now becomes easier as it passes over woodland soil again. Nearing the three-mile point, cross an old logging roadbed. Just when things were getting easy, you hit the boulders again, although not as profuse as before. Upon exiting the boulders the trail becomes more civil, following the hillside much like a contour line. At 3.15 miles the trail turns right at a point of land with a rocky outcrop. The Caney Fork River can be seen here through the open woods of winter. At 3.35 miles the trail rises up to a limestone outcrop. After outlining a rocky hollow and meandering along the hillside, the trail straightens. At 3.6 miles, among a stand of shagbark hickory, arrive at the east end of the Virgin Falls Loop Trail (signs here denote the fact).

Virgin Falls Loop Trail: Hiking the loop in a counterclockwise direction, the trail runs level for 300' then dips. Flanked by scenic bluffs on the right, the treadway becomes significantly more rocky. The trail turns downhill to the left and meanders, then at 3.9 miles arrives at the Falls and Sink of Sheep Cave which are seen 100' to the right.

This waterfall cascades for 10-12' then flows back into the rock only to reappear and fall into the sink. The sinkhole is huge (60 by 80'). The cliffs atop the falls rise for 60'. Cross a land bridge of sorts in front of the falls and take a steep side trail for 375' up their left side. Notice how the creek flows out of the mouth of this cave.

127

Back on the loop trail, which from this point bends sharply left, pass between large boulders and parallel a depression that would be the creek's bed were it not for the sinkhole. At 3.95 miles the trail bends sharply right and switchbacks into the hollow of another dry streambed. Climbing steeply out of the hollow, the trail levels at 4.1 miles. In .15 of a mile the trail makes a long bend right and descends slightly to a point where the thunder of Virgin Falls resonates through the woods. At 4.4 miles turn right at a fire ring from which the trail treads up a small cut in the earth. Just ahead (4.45 miles) the loop trail turns left and leads to the Virgin Fall's viewing area 130' away. A side trail on the right here, leads to the very interesting top area. To gain a thorough understanding of the falls, visit the top area first.

Take the dogleg side trail and pass through a beautiful boulder slide en route to the top area, 800' away. At the top, cross a small land bridge 100' upstream from the fall's cliff. From this bridge you can see into the mouth of the cave from which the creek flows. There are high bluffs above the cave and large boulders that have split and fallen away from its cliffs. Exiting the cave, the creek flows wide and straight for 100', then spills over the cliff. Falling 110', its waters are received and vanish in a large sinkhole.

When seen from the viewing area, the falls are 20-25' wide with the left side of their fall broken by a boulder outcrop at the midpoint. The right half of this powerful beauty plunges the full 110' into the sink.

The falls face northeast. An overcast day is best for photography because of harsh shadows cast by a slightly higher mountain to the southwest. Keystoning is not a problem here because you view them at their midsection.

Leaving the falls, the loop trail bends sharply left and descends a hollow that was probably the creek's bed before it made its way underground. The trail soon treads a firebreak and descends a point of land rather steeply on the east side of the hollow, then treads in the low point of the hollow itself. Pass through a barbed wire fence, then at 4.7 miles arrive at a fire ring and a Y intersection with a roadbed in the river bottom. The loop trail turns left at this three-way intersection and treads the old roadbed (the road on the right leads to private property). At 4.8 miles the trail turns left and leaves the roadbed and bottom land and heads up through a prominent boulder-covered slope. The trail is hard to locate initially but soon becomes much easier to follow as it winds uphill through the boulders. The boulders give way to terrain more conducive to hiking and the trail crosses to the river side of the ridge. Soon, the steep-inclining trail traverses the broadening crest of the ridge and at the five-mile point ties back into the loop's beginning.

Creekside Trail: Hiking upstream this trail initially hits rugged boulders and leads steeply uphill before moderating. Along the creek are clear-green pools and beautiful views of boulders up the streambed. In one spot I found the creekbed dry, then further up the drainage the small sinkhole where it had disappeared. In the same area there are scenic trailside rock overhangs. Soon the trail turns steeply up steps and bends right to pass through medium-size boulders. Exiting the boulders onto more moderate ground, at slightly more than .3 of a mile tie back into the Main Trail taken on the way in.

Ozone Area

Ozone Falls State Natural Area, Cumberland County, Tennessee

Roads: Paved   A "10" 60'   No hiking map needed.
U.S.G.S. Quadrangles: Ozone, Roddy, Tn.
700', side view easy, base difficult because of rubble and steepness

Directions: If driving east on I-40 from the Crossville area, take exit 329 (the Battown Road exit). Drive north and in less than .1 of a mile turn right (east) onto U.S. 70 and zero your odometer. Pass under I-40 at .8 of a mile and after driving

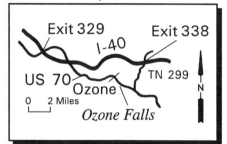

a total of 4.55 miles arrive at the parking area on the right (just before crossing the bridge over Fall Creek). The parking area, near the community of Ozone, is clearly marked. The trail to the base of the falls is on the right.

Alternate directions: If driving west on I-40 from the Harriman area, take exit 338 (the Hwy. 299 exit). Drive south on 299 for 2.85 miles and intersect U.S. 70 at a T intersection. Turn right (west) and drive 4.45 miles to the Ozone Fall's parking area which is on the left.

Note: I purposely left out directions to the top because of the potential danger lurking there. If a child broke and ran from its parents, or if you leaned over the edge a little too far, it would have tragic results. Please see this grand spot from the midpoint or base.

As the trail enters the woods it treads the high level ground above Hwy. 70's cut. Paralleling the roadway and separated from it by only a thin strip of woods, in 250' the trail starts descending. At 320' descend some rock steps and arrive at a rock wall next to the highway. The trail now turns sharply left and descends more rock steps and rubble into the alcove, passing under the shelf-like overhang. Seen here is a perfect example of the softer layers of rock being removed by erosive forces, leaving the unsupported caprock to collapse onto the floor beneath the overhang or tumble into the cove. Small caves are prevalent in this area also. At 500' reach a point where the trail levels. You may continue straight ahead for a side view of the falls, or take the steep pathway on the right to the base.

The path to the base turns downhill over rubble through a forest of chestnut oak, hemlock, and poplar. In 160' cross the cleated trunk of a fallen hemlock then descend still further to the large boulders below the plunge pool.

The falls leap off the sandstone overhang and plunge 60' as a single column of water. The eye is immediately drawn to its outstanding blue-green plunge pool.

Ozone Falls has a huge alcove with striking cliffs of 100' on the right and 85' on the left. The creek has cut a V-shaped channel into the caprock from which it falls. The circular plunge pool is 60' across, its depth is anybody's guess. When viewed from the base, the falls are beautifully framed by large boulders with catawba and sweet birch overhanging the creek as it exits the plunge pool. Lichen covering the sandstone amphitheater walls gives them a slate-gray appearance. The slope on the left is littered with talus. Look for a cave approximately 80° right of the falls at approximately 2:30 vertically. Still further right, the slopes are covered in rhododendron. Looking downstream the creek cascades and pools out of sight through an awesome setting of large boulders.

Spring City Area

Piney Falls State Natural Area, Rhea County, Tennessee

Roads: Paved   A "10"
U.S.G.S. Quadrangle: Spring City, Tn.
White blazed, 1.9 miles round trip, moderate

Directions: From the intersection of U.S. 27 and Tn. Hwy. 68 in Spring City, drive north on Hwy. 68 for 5.05 miles to the community of Grandview. Turn left onto Firetower Road (a brick schoolhouse is located on the northwest corner of this intersection) and drive 1.55 miles to a dirt road which leaves the pavement with a hard right turn. Park here.

Note: The first .5 of a mile of this hike is through private property. The owner has been kind enough to let us pass.

There are two falls here but only one is safe to visit.

The roadbed which serves as our access to the Piney Falls Loop Trail makes a hard right off the paved road and descends. In 350' the road bends left, ascends, then bends right to round the mountain. At .2 of a mile top the ridge. There's a confusing woodland road on the right here. Stay left. Turn downhill and pass under

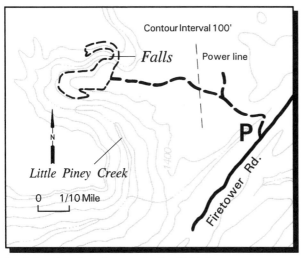

a power line, then re-enter the woods as you near .3 of a mile. The road bends in an S fashion as it bottoms out then rises to cross into the natural area. At .6 of a mile the road dead ends at a picnic area and fire ring. The Piney Falls Loop Trail begins here.

Hiking in a clockwise direction, the trail leads level and southwesterly for 130' then turns westerly. Seven tenths of a mile into the hike pass under a small sandstone bluff where the trail turns sharply left to switchback down the steep slope. At .8 of a mile, the trail levels somewhat at the base of the bluffs and in a long bend right heads north while undulating along their base. At some points these bluffs reach a height of 40'. At .9 of a mile the trail climbs, tops out, then descends into the laurel and rhododendron. Nearing the 1 mile point, the bluffs increase in size. Veiled through the trees, the high rock walls of the fall's amphitheater come into view straight ahead. As you round a protruding cliff that forms the southernmost point of the amphitheater, the falls come in sight.

The falls are housed in a 200'-wide cirque with cliffs of 100' on the left and 60' on the right. Hemlock and laurel thrive in the deep shade of the cove's south side. Set against the contrasting greens of the rimtop forest, the alcove's gray cliffs are streaked brown by algae living in constant moisture.

The trail continues behind the falls and outlines the alcove as it leads to a better vantage point on the north side. During periods of high water you'll get wet passing behind them. On my winter visit, the pebbles lying in the mist behind the falls were glazed with ice (like walking over ball bearings).

After a sheer 50' drop, the falls splash onto stratified rock then cascade into the plunge pool. With its adequate water, and greenery to tone down the starkness, spring is the best time to visit and photograph this beautiful spot.

Return Portion of Loop

Note: If you have no climbing skills, or if ice is encountered, it's best to leave this portion alone and return the way you came in.

Leaving the falls, the trail soon turns uphill. At 1.1 miles pass between a large hemlock on the left, and a large white pine on the right. Turn up the cliffs and ascend the 45° incline from ledge to ledge as it zigzags up to the rim 130' away.

This is a confusing spot and people easily miss the unmarked turnoff up the cliffs. (If you ascend a point of land [the north point of the cirque] then descend its far slope and turn right you've missed the turn.)

Atop the rim, turn right—the trail passes through thick laurel while skirting the cliffs. After passing by the top of the falls at 1.2 miles, the trail bends right and descends to creek level. In 200' cross the creek on large boulders just upstream from the falls. From this point the trail leads uphill and slightly left through the rhododendron, laurel, and pines for just over 400' to complete the loop.

Etowah Area

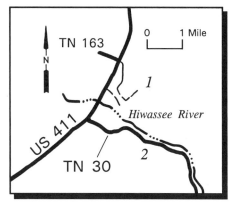

Directions: From the intersection of U.S. 411 and Tn. Hwy. 310 in Etowah, drive south on 411 to the following points of interest:

1. Access to the Falls on Gee Creek: approximately 5.5 miles.

2. Tn. Hwy. 30, access to Lowry Falls: approximately 7.5 miles.

1. Falls on Gee Creek, Polk County, Tennessee

Roads: Graveled   A "5"
U.S.G.S. Quadrangles: Etowah, Oswald Dome, Tn., in their margins
Trail #191, white blazed, 1.1 miles, water crossings, easy-moderate

Directions: In the community of Wetmore, where Tn. Hwy. 163 turns right to go west, turn *left* (east) onto an unmarked paved road. (A sign approaching this road on 411 states "Gee Creek Wilderness.") In .1 of a mile cross the CSX Railroad tracks and bear right. The road now follows the tracks until the odometer reads 1.4 miles where it veers sharply left and away from them. Upon entering the Cherokee National Forest the road surface changes to gravel. Drive a total of 2.2 miles to the Gee Creek information board and trailhead that lie straight ahead.

The road serving as the trail enters the woods over jeep mounds and passes through a mix of pine and hardwoods. The trail's surface is littered with baseball-to softball-size rocks that detract slightly from an otherwise easy to moderate ascent. At the quarter-mile point, Gee Creek, which is heard from the outset, now comes into sight. A confusing spot awaits the unwary hiker at .4 of a mile: the trail continues up the roadbed on the *left*, passing a dead-end pathway that veers right and descends an old jeep road to a creekside camping spot.

The roadbed serving as the trail forks at .45 of a mile. Take the right fork (the Gee Creek Trail) which drops downhill to cross the creek on a footbridge in 130'. Now on the south side of Gee Creek, the treadway ascends out of the creek bottom and at the half-mile point enters the wilderness area as it passes the trail register. At .6 of a mile pass the concrete abutment of an old trestle. The creek runs fast here. The trail bends right and ascends steeply for a short distance. At .7 of a mile notice the beautiful rock bluffs on both sides of the creek, then pass a pre-Civil War concrete flume through which the creek flows and most likely

133

overflows during periods of high water. This was built by the Tennessee Copper Company to power a rock crusher for an iron mining venture. The trail narrows significantly here and becomes very rocky.

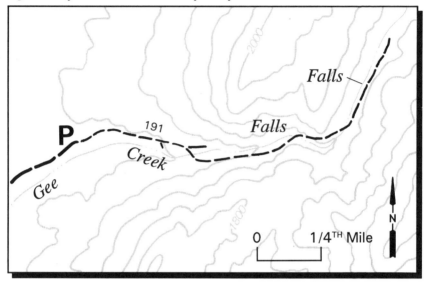

Eight tenths of a mile into the hike, the trail crosses to the left (north) side of Gee Creek between a set of 10' falls. The lower falls are seen as you approach this crossing. The upper falls, known locally as "Blue Hole," are seen as you cross the creek. Blue Hole is the more picturesque of the two, falling through a U-shaped split in the rustic rock face. The left side of the punge pool has large boulders from which to view them.

After having ascended alongside the falls, at just over .85 of a mile cross to the right side of the creek over layers of uplifted bedrock. At .95 of a mile the trail veers right to circumvent large boulders. High bluffs flank both sides of the creek and a camping area located here. The bluffs become more impressive as you venture upstream and view them looking downstream. Pass a small chute-type cascade flowing through a V in the creekbed. I ended my hike at 1.1 miles at another very nice two-tier waterfall. The scenic rock surrounding this waterfall is cleft and tilted 45°. Published accounts say there are no other spectacular waterfalls. The trail makes several more stream crossings and ends at mile 1.9.

2. Lowry Falls,
Polk County, Tennessee

Roads: Paved   A "2"
U.S.G.S. Quadrangle: Oswald Dome, Tn.
Trail #168, white blazed, .25 of a mile, moderate-difficult

Directions: From the intersection of U.S. 411 and Tn. Hwy. 30 East, take Hwy. 30 east for 2.5 miles to the unmarked parking area on the right. (There's a large double culvert seen from Hwy. 30 through which Lowry Branch flows— if crossed, you've gone too far.) The fall's trail begins on the right side of the parking area.

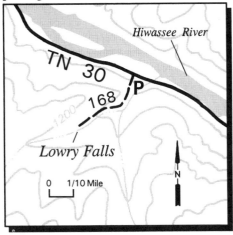

The trail ascends a jeep road for 285' then levels. In another 100' the trail turns steeply uphill. The jeep road ends as it makes this second ascent. At 720' the trail turns right at the confluence of the fall's branch and Left Prong (on the left). (There is an inaccessible waterfall on Left Prong that may be seen from this juncture.) Solomon's seal grows densely here and trillium may be found in lesser amounts.

From the confluence, the trail is much more rugged. Ascending Lowry Branch at a moderate to difficult rate, soon pass the small and obscured lower falls. At .2 of a mile the trail turns right to switchback up and over a large sandstone outcrop. At the midpoint of this switchback take a level pathway leading left, which passes under the overhanging outcrop. In 50' arrive at a viewing area at the base of the middle falls.

Running 70 to 80' as a series of cascades, this is the more scenic of the three falls. To the south of this waterfall is a beautiful sandstone bluff supporting hemlock, chestnut oak, and maple.

To reach the upper falls, climb the switchback and pass a side view of the middle falls. Many windfalls are encountered in the trail's remaining 200' en route to the upper falls.

The upper falls are a series of broken cascades approximately 10' in height. Standing beside them the bluffs above the Hiwassee River may be seen to the northeast.

Ocoee Area

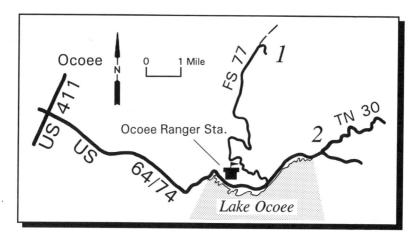

Directions: From the intersection of U.S. Hwys. 64/74 and 411 in the community of Ocoee (east of Cleveland), drive east on U.S. 64/74 for 7.5 miles to the Ocoee Ranger Station. Additional driving directions (given in the text below) are from the ranger station.

Long a favorite with local river runners, the Ocoee River is being put on the map in a big way. This white-water river was chosen as the 1996 Olympic Kayaking venue.

1. Benton Falls,
Polk County, Tennessee

Roads: Paved   An "8" 40'
U.S.G.S. Quadrangle: Oswald Dome, Tn.,   U.S. fee area
Trail #131,   blue blazed, 1.65 miles, easy, open all year

Directions: From the Ocoee Ranger Station, take U.S. 64/74 east for .05 of a mile (250') to Oswald Dome Road (F.S. 77). Turn left and drive 7.55 miles to the Chilhowee Campground/Benton Falls turnoff. Turn right and drive .6 of a mile to the parking area for Benton Falls. The trail begins at the information board. There are two paved trails here. The one on the left leads through the picnic area. To avoid the confusion of hiking through the picnic area, hike the trail on the *right* with the following directions.

From the information board, the Benton Falls Trail leads to the right of the restrooms and in 230' T intersects with the lake's shoreline where it turns left. At approximately 400' (at the near [north] end of the dam) the trail turns left and then right to parallel the backside of the dam. After crossing a small creek the trail ascends. Two tenths of a mile from the trailhead, the Mc Camey Lake and Chilhowee Forest Walk trails split to the right while the Benton Falls Trail leads left. The Benton Falls Trail descends gradually, treading on a wide roadbed while passing through open stands of second-growth pine and hardwoods. The forest floor was open during the time of my visit because of a recent fire.

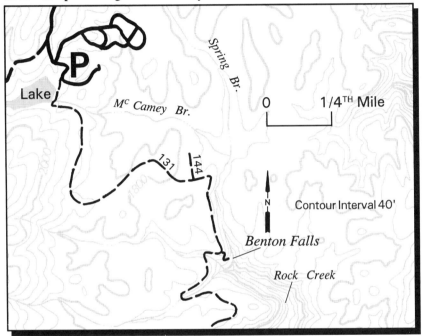

Some of the flowers commonly found here in spring are: bluets, crested dwarf iris, fire pink, yellow jessamine, yellow violets, pinxter flower, and phlox. American holly, maple, and white pine reside here while lesser amounts of hemlock and dogwood are present. Ground covers include galax and partridge-berry. Gray squirrels are everywhere.

Nearing the 1 mile point the roadbed bends right and descends. At 1.15 miles arrive at the intersection of the red-blazed Red Leaf Trail (#144) on the left. The Benton Falls Trail continues straight. At 1.2 miles the trail bends sharply right. In this area there is a great deal of laurel. Just ahead the creek is heard rushing below. At 1.45 miles the rhododendron gets heavier indicating a wetter microclimate. At 1.5 miles arrive at the junction of the Clemmer Mountain Bike Trail.

The Benton Falls Trail turns sharply left and switchbacks down to run alongside the creek. As it passes the top of Benton Falls the trail becomes more rugged, treading over roots and rocks. Leaving the roadbed the trail is narrower and protected by railing. Descend switchbacks and stone steps then at 1.65 miles arrive at the base of this beautiful, stairstepping waterfall.

There are hundreds of steps over which it flows. When I visited, during a dry period, the falls had adequate water and were still very scenic. Sandstone and quartz boulders abound in the shallow plunge pool and range in size up to that of a small car. Where sheltered from the main flow, aquatic plants have taken up residence in its cracked ledges.

2. Falls on Rock Creek, Scenic Spur Trail, Polk County, Tennessee

Roads: Paved   Secret Falls A "10"
U.S.G.S. Quadrangles: Caney Creek, Oswald Dome, Tn.
Trail #78, blue blazed, 1.65 miles, water crossings, moderate

Directions: From the Ocoee Ranger Station, drive east on U.S. 64/74 for 2.25

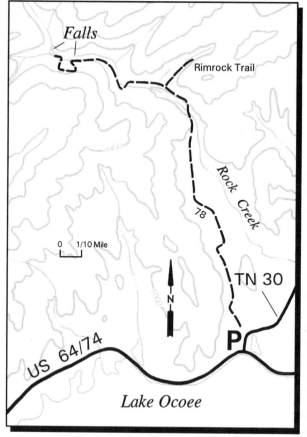

miles and turn left onto Tn. Hwy. 30 West. Drive approximately .05 of a mile (250') to a graveled road on the left. (Directly across Hwy. 30 from a backwater slough of Lake Ocoee.) Take this road for 350' to the parking area. The trail begins at the information board at the south end of the parking area.

Plants and trees to be seen along the trail are: crested dwarf iris (both blue and purple), foamflower, fire pink, and several varieties of trillium. Large oaks, maple, hemlock, and white pine form the canopy with American bladdernut and dogwood as the understory. Thickets of laurel and rhododendron are found in the more moist areas.

With a right turn the Scenic Spur Trail leaves the information board and begins ascending an old roadbed. At 650' the Clemmer Mountain Bike Trail is closely encountered. The Scenic Spur makes a reverse S here and descends to cross the high end of a hollow then turns up to pass through a gap. Topping out, the trail descends and parallels the west side of a hollow that opens to the north. After leveling, the trail bends sharply left at .35 of a mile and the sound of Rock Creek is heard distantly on the right. Descending as its leaves this bend, the trail soon levels. Small colonies of club moss are seen here.

At .65 of a mile leave the large hardwoods and enter the openness of a more youthful forest. Honeysuckle vines climb these smaller trees. Approaching the 1 mile point, the trail bends slightly left and soon joins Rock Creek, gently ascending with, and following closely up its west side. Just ahead the gorge narrows and the mountainsides become very steep. At 1.15 miles cross to the right side of Rock Creek on steppingstones and hike upstream. Just shy of 1.25 miles the Scenic Spur continues straight while the Rimrock Trail branches off to the right. The Scenic Spur ascends at an easy to moderate rate, soon levels, then becomes narrow and rocky. At 1.5 miles the trail appears to dead end at an outcrop of stratified rock. Cross to the left side of the creek where you'll find that the trail bends right and continues upstream, ascending at a moderate rate. At 1.6 miles the lower falls become fully visible below. Loose rock on the slope makes it unsafe to descend to its base. In another 275' arrive at the upper falls and the end of the official trail.

The trail stays perpetually wet and muddy here as the rock wall on the left weeps nutrients to aquatic plants. On your approach, during a spring visit, Jack-in-the-pulpit and Solomon's seal may be seen in bloom in this moist environ. This is the more scenic of the two falls located here, falling 10' through a split in the rock. The rock walls flanking the falls are extremely beautiful with lots of moss covering the left exposure.

For the more skilled hiker, there is a little-known waterfall lying secretly upstream. To reach it, look for a steep pathway at the end of the official trail leading up and under the overhang on the left. This circumvents the rock face. (The pathway is wet and slick here, so be careful.) Once atop the overhang, the pathway levels and leads upstream for approximately 200' through a heavy stand of rhododendron. Where a light boulder slide becomes a heavy one, descend towards creek level using the slide's wash as your pathway. When you arrive at the creek (above the aforementioned upper falls), hike upstream for approximately 150' and view this secluded waterfall and its awesome surroundings from atop one of the large streamside boulders. This is the book's cover shot.

The falls are situated in one of the more rustic and scenic settings in this book. Located on Rock Creek just above its confluence with Laurel Branch, this waterfall is flanked by white pine, hemlock, and laurel, with alder growing in the fissured streamside bedrock. The exposed sandstone bluffs shimmer with traces of quartz.

Farner Area

Turtletown Falls Loop Trail, Polk County, Tennessee

Roads: Graveled   A "3" & "2" respectively
U.S.G.S. Quadrangle: Farner, Tn.
Trail #185,   white blazed,   3.65 miles total,   minor water crossings,
moderate

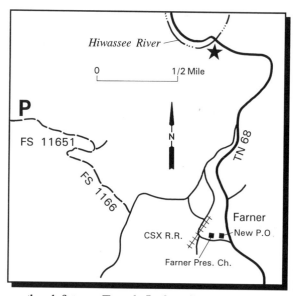

Directions: From the Hwy. 68 bridge over the Hiwassee River, north of the community of Farner, drive south for 1.7 miles and turn right (west) onto Church St. (The new post office and Farner Presbyterian Church are located here.) Zero your odometer and travel west. Cross, veer right, then follow the CSX Railroad tracks. In .35 of a mile turn left onto an unnamed street. Drive .15 of a mile to another left turn. Travel .5 of a mile and turn right onto F.S. 1166. Drive the curvy 1166 for approximately 1 mile and turn left onto the unmarked F.S. 11651. (The Forest Service designates these as two separate roads but I consider them one, as I saw no change.) After driving a total of 1.5 miles from the pavement, ford a small creek. The parking area lies just ahead. The Turtletown Loop Trail begins on the right side of the parking area.

Plants and trees to be seen here include: galax, partridgeberry, mountain laurel, rhododendron, chestnut oak, hemlock, maple, mountain magnolia, crested dwarf iris, fire pink, pink lady's slipper, and painted trillium.

Heading due north on an old jeep road the trail leads steeply uphill. Topping out at 400', the trail bends right then left and descends back to creek level, arriving at a small camping area. For the next half mile the trail is in Turtletown Creek's flood plain and may have wet stretches or be under water after heavy rains. The trail turns sharply uphill at .7 of a mile as you approach the beginning of the loop.

Hike the loop in a clockwise direction (the roadbed on the right is the return

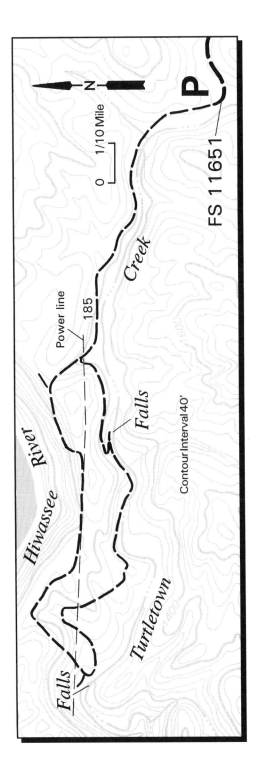

N

0 1/10 Mile

Hiwassee River

Falls

Falls

Power line

185

Creek

Turtletown

Contour Interval 40'

FS 11651

P

portion of the loop). Leaving the roadbed, the trail is now a slim and undulating one that treads the steep mountainside with Turtletown Creek far below. The trail descends and immediately crosses a dripping branch that flows over rock. At .9 of a mile the trail angles right and then outlines a hollow in deeper woods. Nearing the 1 mile point, upon entering another small hollow, the falls become visible approximately 70' in elevation below. There are many windfalls in the Turtletown Gorge and they are especially prevalent as you near the falls. As you descend the second of two switchbacks the beautiful falls come into full view. A side trail at the base of the switchbacks leads upstream for approximately 200' to the fall's viewing area, while the loop trail continues right and downstream.

Turtletown Falls spills in a fall of 15', its flow split in half by bedrock at its top. This waterfall has an amazing resemblance to those of Long Creek, S.C.

The power of Turtletown Creek is very evident as you hike downstream and rejoin the creek. At 1.25 miles the trail leaves the sandy creek bottom and levels slightly above it. Soon thereafter, the trail leaves the creekside altogether and climbs. At 1.45 miles top the base of a small ridge and outline a hollow. For the next .4 of a mile the trail leaves sight of the creek while outlining other hollows high on the mountainside. While descending, at 1.85 miles the trail joins an old roadbed which serves as the return portion of the loop. A side trail (the downhill portion of this roadbed) leads to the top of the lower falls 420' away. Near the top, look for an unmarked pathway leading downstream for 300' to the base area.

The lower falls are a 150' long, 20' high series of cascades shaped like an upside down Y. The creek makes a 90° bend here, running from southeast to southwest.

To complete the loop, return *to* and continue *up* the old roadbed. Three-hundred feet from the fall's side trail (at mile 1.9) the loop trail enters an area of recent logging activity. After passing under a power line reenter the woods and continue ascending this roadbed. The blazes are scarce as there is not a tree large enough to paint. At approximately 2.1 miles, the trail turns easterly after topping the ridge. For the next .4 of a mile the trail undulates along the ridge line, alternating between the woods and power line right of way. At one spot (2.35 miles) the Hiwassee River (to the north) can be seen when the leaves are off. The blazes are more frequent in this area as the trees are larger. At 2.6 miles the roadbed serving as the trail turns sharply left. (There is a side road here leading to the power line which is approximately 200' to the right. Do not take it.) Soon the trail descends while making a long bend right. At 2.7 miles an extension of the loop trail splits left and according to the Forest Service ties back into F.S. 1166. In a low spot from which a small creek rises (2.75 miles) pass a barricade then immediately cross this creek. At 2.85 miles pass under the power line. The trail begins descending steeply here then at 2.9 miles ties back into the beginning portion of the loop, upstream from the falls. A left turn leads back to the parking area.

Tellico Plains Area

Coker Creek Falls,
Polk County, Tennessee

Roads: Graveled   An "8"
U.S.G.S. Quadrangle: Mc Farland, Tn.
Trail #183,   white blazed,   minor water crossings,   835' to base of falls,
2.85 miles to parking at end,   moderate

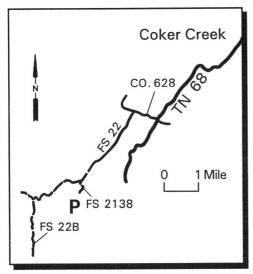

Note: Uprooted trees have opened up gaping holes in many areas along this trail. Also, watch for slick footing on loose chips of slate.

Directions: From the intersection of Tn. Hwys. 165 and 68 in Tellico Plains, drive south on Hwy. 68 for 12.7 miles to County Road 628 (across from the Calvary Baptist Church, approximately 2.15 miles south of the Old Country Store in the community of Coker Creek). Turn right and drive .85 of a mile to Ducketts Ridge Road (County Road 626/F.S. 22). Turn left and continue for 3.0 miles to F.S. 2138. Turn left and travel the remaining .9 of a mile to the parking area and trailhead. The Coker Creek Trail enters the woods on the right (west) side of the parking area at the information board.

Shuttle directions: From the intersection of F.S. 22 and 2138 (the turnoff for Coker Creek Falls), take F.S. 22 south for 1.6 miles to its juncture with F.S. 22B. Drive the often rugged and high clearance 22B for 1.65 miles to the southern terminus of the Coker Creek Trail.

Coker Creek is a very beautiful clear creek that rushes over bedrock and boulders for the entire course of the hike. Its falls cascade and spill over rock ledges in a run of approximately 1000'. At times the creek is deep in the gorge, then at others right next to the trail.

Trees to be seen along this trail are: laurel, hemlock, chestnut oak, mountain magnolia, dogwood, and 100'+ white pines. The pileated woodpecker is often heard proudly calling through this mature forest. Flowers include several varieties of trillium, bluets, crested dwarf iris, fire pink, foamflower, and violets.

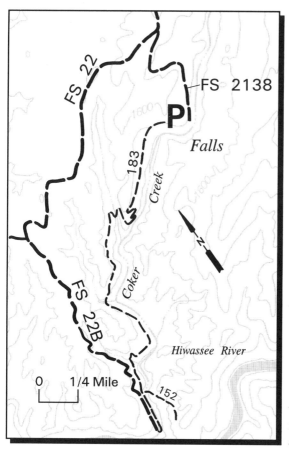

The trail begins level then at 350' turns uphill in the vicinity of the upper tier of Coker Creek Falls. Descending from that point, the trail passes alongside this long series of falls. At .1 of a mile a side trail zigzags to a creekside view of the fall's midpoint.

Back on the main trail, continue descending and at 835' look for a level side trail leading to another view of the falls. At the quarter-mile point the now inaccessible falls end far below the main trail.

At .3 of a mile the trail veers inland and treads an old logging road for a short distance then turns southwesterly in unison with the creek. Descending at a moderate rate, arrive at a creekside camping area at .65 of a mile. The trail now climbs, levels, then at .75 of a mile descends to rejoin the creek.

At .85 of a mile the trail turns uphill. Many windfalls are seen here on both sides of the creek from the now narrow trail. One mile into the hike reach a point of land where the trail descends three switchbacks. Now at creek level, the trail enters a hollow. Foamflower and Solomon's seal line a small creek flowing out of this hollow.

The trail switchbacks out of this hollow and for the most part runs high above Coker Creek, dipping occasionally to join it. At 1.3 miles the trail passes through storm damage which has opened the creek up for viewing and the steep mountainsides to the north and east as well. The views are especially scenic as the trail rounds an open, rocky point. Again, the area is recovering from storm damage with small trees and vines covering the slopes. The trail soon reenters the woodland shade.

The trail descends moderately and at 1.6 miles crosses a small creek. There are three large quartz boulders here to serve as a landmark. This creek is teeming with crawfish and salamanders. Take a break and observe them as they go about their daily hunt for food.

Leaving this creek the trail turns steeply uphill, levels, then gradually descends among the windfalls. Arriving back at creek level at 1.75 miles, the trail now treads (for the moment) an old logging road within 50-100' of a more placid Coker Creek.

At 2.05 miles the trail and creek turn due west. Soon the trail heads towards the hillsides and crosses a small wet-weather branch. Now 100' in elevation above Coker Creek, great distances can be seen to both the south and east. This is another very scenic part of the trail. The trail descends the hillside and at 2.3 miles returns to creek level. (From this point on, for the most part, the trail treads a logging road.) At 2.35 miles the trail turns right and ascends a switchback then outlines a hollow. High above the creek once again, at 2.45 miles the trail descends then levels alongside Coker Creek. At 2.65 miles arrive at the junction of the John Muir Trail (#152) which is on the left. Pass through a primitive camping area and continue downstream on a wide roadbed that bends to the right and ascends to the end parking area at mile 2.85.

Conasauga Falls,
Monroe County, Tennessee

Roads: Graveled   A "9"
U.S.G.S. Quadrangle: Tellico Plains, Tn.
Trail #170, white blazed, .65 of a mile, moderate

Directions: From the intersection of Tn. Hwys. 165 and 68 in Tellico Plains, drive south on Hwy. 68 for 2.35 miles to Old Hwy. 68 (F.S. 341). Turn right and in .5 of a mile pass over a badly rutted stretch of Old Hwy. 68. At 1.1 miles the pavement ends. Continue for a total of 2.4 miles to F.S. 341A. Turn right and drive .55 of a mile to its circular end. The trail to the falls begins on the south side of the parking area.

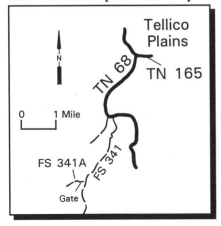

The trail enters the woods and descends at an easy rate. At just over .1 of a mile the trail turns right to round the point of a ridge, then descends at a moderate rate. According to a Forest Service publication this area burned several years ago. Where fire ravaged, wild blueberries and sassafras reside.

145

Much of the slope is planted in pines. Beautiful views of the mountains to the south are to be had through and over the low but growing pines.

At one-quarter mile the trail switchbacks down the mountainside. The distant

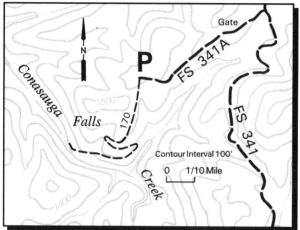

roar of Conasauga Creek can be heard here. As the trail enters a hollow, the forest becomes more diverse with American holly, hemlock, laurel, maple, and rhododendron in its depths. Exiting the hollow, at .55 of a mile the trail joins Conasauga Creek, following it at a distance of 40 to 50'. After passing through a rocky stretch, and where uprooted trees have opened a gaping hole or two in the trail, at .65 of a mile pass the top of the falls. In this moist environ look for large ferns, trillium, Solomon's seal and galax. The trail ends in 130' with a steep descending left turn that accesses the base of the falls.

Conasauga Falls is a super beautiful, three-tier waterfall that runs 40', dropping approximately 25' between the steep hillsides. The main flow is split in half by the irregular form of the rock face. The greenest of mosses grow where sheltered from constant water flow.

Tellico River Drainage

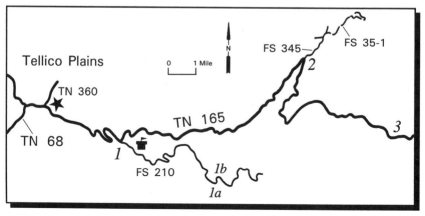

Directions: From the intersection of Tn. Hwys. 68 and 165 in Tellico Plains, drive east on 165 (through the heart of town) for 1.15 miles and intersect Tn. Hwy. 360. From this intersection take Hwy. 165 the following distances to access these points of interest:

1. F.S. 210 (Tellico River Road), access to (a) Bald River and (b) Baby Falls: 4.3 miles.
2. F.S. 345, access to the Falls on the North Fork Citico Creek: 13.6 miles.
3. Rattlesnake Rock (Fall Branch Fall's) parking area: 21.8 miles.

1(a) Bald River Falls, (b) Baby Falls, Monroe County, Tennessee

Roads: Paved   A "9" 60' & A "7" respectively
U.S.G.S. Quadrangle: Bald River Falls, Tenn., N.C.
Seen from the road.

(a) Bald River Falls: Drive the Tellico River Road (F.S. 210) for 6.35 miles to the parking area for the Bald River Trail.

There are several spots from which this huge white-water spectacle may be viewed. The best are from the F.S. 210 bridge below their base, and above them, reached by hiking a steep portion of the Bald River Trail for approximately 700'.

(b) Baby Falls: From the Bald River Fall's parking area, drive F.S. 210 upstream an additional .3 of a mile to a point where this small waterfall is seen from the road. Parking is not allowed beside the falls. Drive .05 of a mile (250') further upstream to the parking area and walk the road back to view them.

This is a small but very scenic waterfall that is popular with kayakers who are frequently seen practicing in the turbulent, swirling waters beneath them. I was very impressed by the beauty of these churning, clear-green waters and the mountainous backdrop.

2. Falls on the North Fork Citico Creek, Monroe County, Tennessee

Roads: Graveled   A "6" 30'
Map: Joyce Kilmer-Slickrock and Citico Creek Wilderness
White blazed, trail #'s 105 and 98, 4.75 miles to falls,
5.6 miles to Cold Springs Gap Trail, potentially deep water crossings,
moderate-difficult

Note: I hiked this trail with the creek at summer levels and found the crossings easily made. I'm sure they would be much more difficult and possibly dangerous during winter or spring. Above the lower falls the trail has many water crossings. However, being this high in the drainage they are shallow. My advice is to end your trek at the lower falls. They are by far the more scenic of the three falls.

If water levels are not too high, this is the perfect day-long springtime hike. This woodland boasts some of the most diverse flora that I've encountered. Plant varieties found along the trail include large colonies of bluets, crested dwarf iris, foamflower, hearts a bustin' (euonymus), many varieties of trillium, pink lady's slipper, showy orchis, Solomon's seal, white and blue violets, and partridgeberry. Trees found here include: hemlock, rhododendron, mountain magnolia, mountain laurel, maple, poplar, and oak.

For general photography the hike up Citico Creek is especially beautiful when flatly lit. This condition brings out the best in its slate-gray rock.

Directions: From Hwy. 165 turn left onto F.S. 345 (sign: Indian Boundary Recreation Area). In 1.25 miles veer right onto F.S. 35-1 whereupon the road changes to gravel. After driving 3.6 miles from 165 look for a dirt road on the right (F.S. 40480) which is also the trailhead. There may be a carsonite stake here identifying the trail as #105 (South Fork Citico Trail). This serves as the connector to #98 (the North Fork Trail). (If you miss the trailhead there is a campground 250' further down 35-1 on the right.)

The trail begins as F.S. 40480 splits to the right from F.S. 35-1 in a Y-type configuration. The roadbed serving as the trail leads uphill and right as it passes over the foot of a ridge, then descends while outlining the mountainside. At 700' the roadbed gives way to a single-lane footpath that soon passes a concrete structure on the left. (There are several locations in the first mile where evidence of a long abandoned Warden camp are seen.)

At the quarter-mile point, the trail crosses a small branch then undulates high on the slopes above Citico Creek. The trail descends, levels, and crosses a small creek then winds through an overgrown fruit orchard. At .55 of a mile enter into the Citico Creek Wilderness and sign up at the trail register.

From this point the trail treads an old logging railroad bed beside Citico Creek at an easy rate. After passing through a saddle-type gap, at .85 of a mile the trail splits: the South Fork Trail leads right and the North Fork Trail veers left to cross an iron footbridge. Now on the North Fork Citico Trail, cross the footbridge just above the confluence of the North and South Forks of Citico Creek. (Henceforth, the North Fork of Citico Creek is referred to as Citico Creek.)

At .95 of a mile pass a small dam and just upstream a nonfunctional overhead cable car. Some of the creek's bedrock in this area is pockmarked and swirlholed. Large rounded boulders in the creek are testament to its power, having been tumbled downstream.

At 1.3 miles make the first of many water crossings, this time to the north side

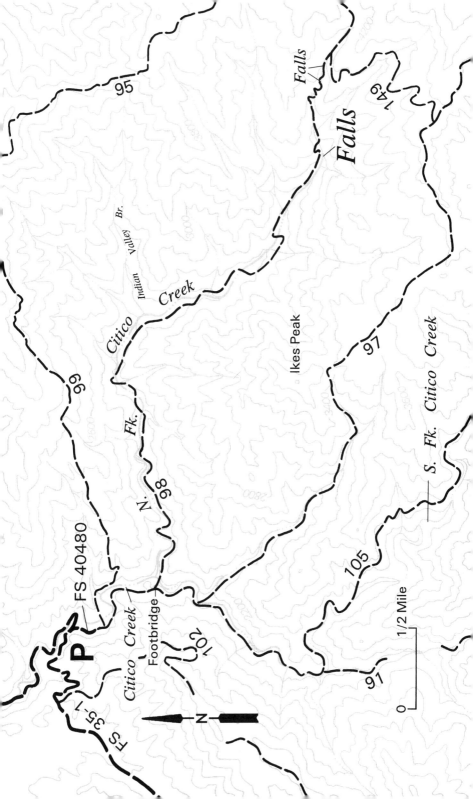

Falls

Falls

95

149

97

Ikes Peak

S. Fk. Citico Creek

Br.

Valley

Indian

Citico Creek

N. Fk.

86

105

99

FS 40480

P

Citico Creek

Footbridge

102

16

FS 35-1

N

0   1/2 Mile

of the creek. In another .1 of a mile cross back to the right side of the creek near a fire ring. After cresting a rise, the trail levels and bends in unison with the creek.

Nearing the two mile point pass on top of a succession of four small islands. The islands were not cut off from dry land at the time of my hike, but would be during periods of high water. At 2.1 miles the trail is again forced closer to the creek, this time by a small bluff. At 2.2 miles cross to the left side of the creek. At 2.35 miles pass through a camping area, then cross to the right side of Citico Creek. After crossing another small tributary, pass through a wet spot with crossties still in place. At a dead-end rock outcrop, 2.55 miles into the hike, the trail crosses to the creek's left side then immediately recrosses to its right. (There is also a route along the rock outcrop. If you're careful you can negotiate your way through it and avoid this double crossing. These are deep crossings and there were no good rocks to cross on during my visit.)

Nearing the three mile point the trail passes over the length of an island. Again, this crossing would be a problem during high water as the island shows signs of having been under water. The trail now ascends at a little steeper rate (easy to moderate). At 3.3 miles the trail crosses to the left side of the creek and soon passes through a wet stretch where a small rocky branch flows into Citico Creek. After passing a midstream island at 3.75 miles, cross to the right side of Citico Creek. The official map shows the trail in error here as switchbacking up the slope on the left side of the creek. Instead, the trail climbs steeply, dips and rises sharply in quick succession, then crosses to Citico Creek's north side diagonally on an island. Evidence of the railroad diminishes here.

On the creek's north side, at 4.1 miles arrive at a fire ring where the trail switchbacks out of the creek bottom's impassable boulders for the relative ease of deeper woods. Top the switchback in 100'. From the last crossing the terrain is much more rugged and the creek now tumbles well below trail level. At 4.25 miles turn back towards the creek in an area of large boulders. There are two prominent boulders on the left near the point where the creek splits. Cross the left branch just above its confluence with the right fork, and continue up the left side of the right fork. From this point the trail progressively steepens. At 4.7 miles, pass a prominent boulder outcrop on the left side of the trail. Four and three-quarter miles into the hike arrive at a point beside the falls. They may be seen from the trail when the leaves are off.

To reach the base, look for an 18" tree stump standing 2 1/2' high in the middle of the trail, with its sawn trunk fallen towards the creek. A slim pathway on the upstream side of the trunk descends the steep slope. Work your way through the streamside laurel and hemlock and in 150' arrive at the base of the falls.

The creek flows through a V in the rock then drops 30' in two tiers. The rock wall on the left is 35' high and covered in toadskin lichen and beautiful moss. Mosses more thickly cover the moist rock on the shaded right side and the boulders at the base as well. Fallen tree trunks mixed among the boulders add

150

to its beauty. The fall's cove has dense rhododendron and atop its rim are large hemlocks. A small plunge pool at its base holds thousands of flat, rounded rocks.

Back on the main trail the hike continues upstream, first climbing a steep switchback alongside the falls. After passing two small waterfalls, one at 5.4 miles, and the other at 5.5 miles, the North Fork Trail ties into the Cold Spring Gap Trail (#149) at 5.6 miles (400' upstream from the third waterfall found on this creek). If you blinked your eyes you'd miss this intersection.

3. Fall Branch Falls,
Monroe County, Tennessee

Roads: Paved   A "10" 60'
Map: Joyce Kilmer-Slickrock and Citico Creek Wilderness
Trail #87, 1.3 miles, minor water crossing, difficult

I have visited this location in the both the wet and dry months—is it ever a beauty. On my fall visit there wasn't much water so I arranged to come back after

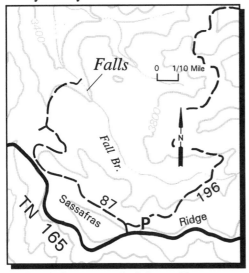

normal winter rains for a real show. I got much more than I bargained for. This time there was so much water that it was hard to get close enough to photograph them. Like smoke from a campfire, the spray followed my every move. (I guess spray follows beauty, too!) Also, every boulder was coated in a treacherous glaze of ice making it impossible to reach where I had stood months earlier.

Directions: At this location look for the Rattlesnake Rock parking area on the left. The trail begins at the west end of the parking area.

Alternate Directions: From Beech Gap, which is on the North Carolina - Tennessee line, drive west on Hwy. 165 for 1.5 miles to the Rattlesnake Rock parking area, on the right.

As you enter the woods the trail (an old roadbed) passes through knee- to waist-high growth. In 225' arrive at the trail register. Here, the Falls Branch Trail veers left and the Jeffrey Hell Trail (#196) leads to the right.

The Falls Branch Trail parallels the north face of Sassafras Ridge for .3 of a mile then bends left. Slightly more than .4 of a mile into the hike arrive at a confusing pathway on the right. This leads to a small knob. Stay left here and pass through a saddle-type gap.

At the half-mile point the trail runs close to Hwy. 165 then bends right to round the mountain. Soon the trail bends left as it outlines a cove. As you exit this bend, look very carefully to the right for the trail which now leaves this old roadbed. (A pathway here leads straight ahead to tie into Hwy. 165.) For further verification look for a large (3′ in diameter) trailside hemlock standing 30′ north of the old roadbed. When I visited the falls this tree had a faded white arrow painted on it pointing the way.

Take the trail over the rise passing by the hemlock. On the downslope you'll encounter lots of loose rock and roots galore. Three tenths of a mile from the old roadbed, cross Fall Branch and pass through a split boulder. The trail leads upstream another 300′ to the base of the falls.

This waterfall rains down from a showy cirque-like cliff. This exposure is at least 250′ across. Its adequate year-round flow is surprising for a creek so close to the ridge line.

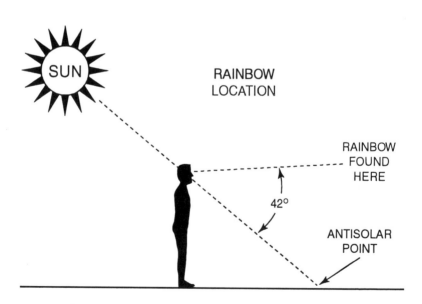

Toccoa Area

Toccoa Falls, Stephens County, Ga.

186' An "8" No hiking map needed   Private Fee Area
Located on the campus of Toccoa Falls College

Directions: From the intersection of U.S. 123/Ga. Hwy. 365 and Ga. Hwy.

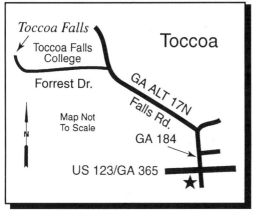

184 (N. Broad St.), in downtown Toccoa, drive north on N. Broad St. (the route soon changes to Ga. Hwy. Alt. 17 North), and in .45 of a mile arrive at the traffic light intersection with Falls Road. Turn left and drive 1.15 miles to Forrest Dr. (sign: Toccoa Falls College). Turn left and travel another .85 of a mile (passing through the Toccoa Falls College security gate enroute) to the Gate Cottage Gift Shop, (which is beneath the restaurant). The falls are accessed by passing through the gift shop where a small fee is collected.

Exit the upstream end of the cottage and hike a graveled trail for 600' to the base of the falls.

Beauty and Tragedy

"Toccoa" is the Cherokee word for beautiful, and during certain times of year it is exceptionally so. The best photos I've seen are of the falls in a snowy, wintry setting with the blue sky as a backdrop.

In November 1977, an earthen dam impounding a 40 acre lake, on the creek above the falls, burst after torrential rains, flooding the campus and taking the lives of 39 persons, while they slept.

Tallulah Falls Area

Stonewall Falls, Rabun County, Ga.

Roads: Graveled/High Clearance   A "5" 15'   US Fee Area
U.S.G.S. Quadrangle: Tiger, Ga.
Seen from parking area   See Area Map under Tallulah Gorge State Park

---

Directions: From the U.S. 441 bridge, over the Tallulah River, in the town of Tallulah Falls, drive north on 441 for 6.7 miles to W. Boggs Mountain Road. Turn left and travel .3 of a mile to Old U.S. 441. With a left turn, drive .45 of a mile to F.S. 20. Turn right and drive 1.75 miles (passing the Stonewall Falls Mountain Bike Trail parking area at 1.3 miles) to a fork. Take the right fork for 200' to the parking area and falls.

This magnificent waterfall needs our help. The parking area doubles as a primitive campsite. Instead of hauling out their refuse, uncaring campers burn items thinking that they'll disappear. Melted aluminum cans and plastics fill the fire ring.

Tallulah Gorge State Park

Park hours 8:00 a.m. to dark (gates locked)   Emergency: 911
Telephone: (706) 754-7970   Camping reservations: (706) 754-7979

"The cataract of Niagara and its great whirlpool and banks, is the only superior natural curiosity to the Rapids of Tallulah, that I have ever seen."
-- Georgia Journal, September 1819

The most wondrous of Georgia's falls reside in Tallulah Gorge State Park. The names of its falls suggest both great power (Tempesta, Hurricane and

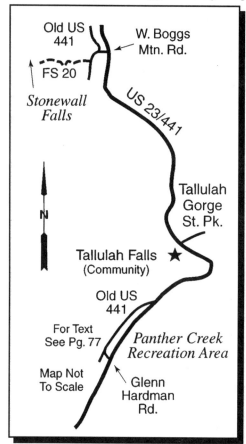

Oceana) and romance (L' Eau d' Or [a.k.a. *La Dore*, French for *water of gold*] and Bridal Veil). Once, the mighty Tallulah River flowed freely, carving a deep and scenic gorge. Dammed just above the gorge, most of its waters were diverted for power generation to fill the electrical needs of a booming Atlanta and northeast Georgia. Prior to the dam's construction (completed in 1913) the falls were a major attraction and considered the "Niagara of the South." The town of Tallulah Falls had fine accomodations and the Tallulah Falls Railroad brought in the tourists. On two occasions, gorge promoters hired aerialists to cross it. Professor Leon made his hair-raising walk on July 24, 1886. During his crossing, a stabilizing rope snapped. The crowd horrified, and his face livid with fear, he finished only half of his proposed round-trip walk. The most publicized crossing was made by Karl Wallenda on July 18, 1970. The towers that held his wire are still in place, though the north tower lays on its side.

Tallulah Gorge has been a scenic attraction for over 150 years. Early visitors endured great hardship, traveling many days or even weeks over primitive roads to reach this once remote natural wonder. I am intrigued by its human and geologic history. Cut into solid quartz, gorge depth varies from 250', below the dam (site of the *now* non-existent Arrowhead Rapids) to 750' at overlook #1, on the north rim. If measuring the gorge's depth from the bluff that lies to the east of the north Wallenda Tower (near overlook #1), it is more than 1000' deep.

In 1911, an age when man was mastering nature in every way, the most hotly contested environmental battle of its day was waged to keep the river flowing free. The leader of this fight was Helen Dortch Longstreet, the young, second wife of Civil War Lt. Gen. James Longstreet. Mrs. Longstreet led the Tallulah Falls Conservation Association in a vain effort against the predecessor of Georgia Power and *then* Gov. Brown, spending her time and fortune to stop the damming of the Tallulah River. The park's trail system is named in her honor.

My introduction to Tallulah Gorge was in the mid-1970's. At that time, I was completely turned off by the carnival-like shops and accesses that crowded the gorge's south rim. State park status has been a definite plus. First, it is now a much safer place to visit. Entry into the Gorge, to visit either Hurricane or Sliding Rock (Bridal Veil Falls) is by permit only. This is with good reason. Before the permit system, many novice hikers were hurt or died as a result of accidents in the gorge. Permitting has reduced accidents to near zero, as hikers are made aware of the dangers. Second, visitors are made more aware of the gorge's sensitive environment: The park's rare plants and animals (some found only here) enjoy a zone of protection.

Tallulah Gorge is the crown jewel in Georgia's state park system. It would also qualify as being the state's "Waterfall Park," for it contains 6 full-time waterfalls, and 2 part-timers (waterfalls of the wet-weather variety). Located to the north and east of the historic town of Tallulah Falls, its 3,000 acres hold some of Georgia's most striking scenery. Designated a state park in 1992, this unit operates through a unique cooperative effort between the Georgia Department of Natural Resources and the Georgia Power Company.

Visiting the Park

There is something here for everyone. From a short, leisurely walk, to an arduous hike. From camping, to kayaking. From swimming at the 63 acre Tallulah Falls Lake, to water sliding at Bridal Veil Falls. From bird watching, to rock climbing (permit required). There are even tennis courts.

Plan to spend at least a full day. This would be a mere introduction. Before hitting the trail, visit the Jane Hurt Yarn Interpretive Center for an intimate overview. After the exhibits, be sure to see the award-winning, 20 minute

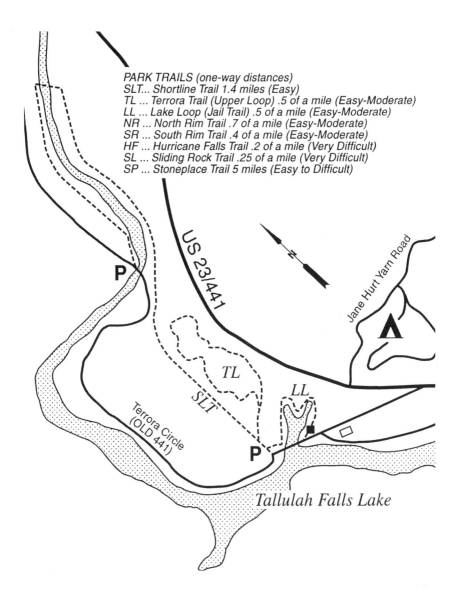

PARK TRAILS (one-way distances)
SLT... Shortline Trail 1.4 miles (Easy)
TL ... Terrora Trail (Upper Loop) .5 of a mile (Easy-Moderate)
LL ... Lake Loop (Jail Trail) .5 of a mile (Easy-Moderate)
NR ... North Rim Trail .7 of a mile (Easy-Moderate)
SR ... South Rim Trail .4 of a mile (Easy-Moderate)
HF ... Hurricane Falls Trail .2 of a mile (Very Difficult)
SL ... Sliding Rock Trail .25 of a mile (Very Difficult)
SP ... Stoneplace Trail 5 miles (Easy to Difficult)

US 23/441

Jane Hurt Yarn Road

TL

SLT

LL

Terrora Circle
(OLD 441)

Tallulah Falls Lake

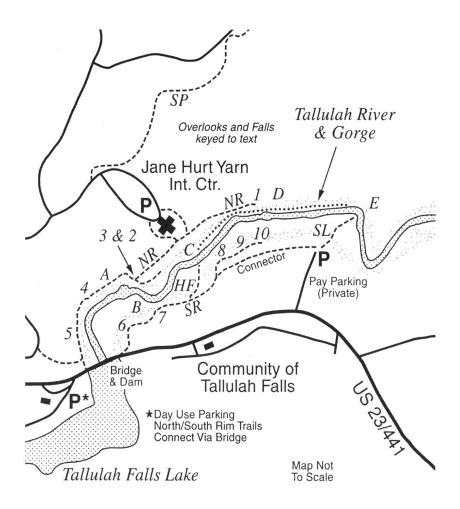

SP

*Overlooks and Falls
keyed to text*

Tallulah River & Gorge

Jane Hurt Yarn
Int. Ctr.

P

NR 1 D

E

3 & 2

NR

C

8 9 10

SL

A

4

HF

Connector

P

5

B

6 7

SR

Pay Parking
(Private)

Bridge
& Dam

P*

Community of Tallulah Falls

US 23/441

*Day Use Parking
North/South Rim Trails
Connect Via Bridge

Tallulah Falls Lake

Map Not
To Scale

documentary for gorge views that only a bird has. If time is limited, hike the north and south rim trails, but make it a point to come back, for the best of the best lies within the gorge. The more inquisitive visitor may want to join one of the ranger-led hikes (call ahead for dates and times).

Twice a year, spring and fall, the Tallulah River is allowed to flow at its pre-dam levels (500 to 700 Cubic Feet per Second). During these scheduled water releases, a limited number of experienced kayakers are permitted to put in below the third fall (Hurricane) and shoot Oceana, Bridal Veil, Sweet Sixteen, and the remaining rapids. Park visitors are not permitted within the gorge during these water releases. However, one may watch the "boaters" go over Oceana from overlook #1. Most of them study this Class 5 waterfall carefully, in an upstream pool, trying to gain their nerve. It seems no matter how careful their plan, they are at its mercy.

Going over the fall's right side (as viewed from the overlook) they are forced to its left side where most boaters disappear in the throes of a hydraulic. After a few seconds, that seem like an eternity, they reemerge, whereupon excited onlookers breathe a collective sigh of relief.

Viewing the Falls

By far, most visitors see Tallulah's falls from the overlooks accessed via the rim trails. Four of the park's main falls are visible from the rim. The following are the overlook locations that provide those views. Italicized numbers (overlooks) and letters (waterfalls) are keyed to the map.

1. Oceana *(D)*, seen far below.

2 & 3. Frontal view of L' Eau d' Or and Hawthorne Pool *(A)*.

2 & 7. Tempesta *(B)*, viewed far below.

8. Hurricane *(C)*, seen far below.

9. Hurricane *(C)*, Oceana *(D)*, and Caledonia Cascade (wet-weather fall near overlook #*1* on North Rim).

10. Caledonia Cascade seen across gorge.

Bridal Veil Falls *(E)* is seen from within the gorge. A full view of Hurricane and Oceana is also available while hiking in the gorge.

Gorge Floor Access

Both gorge access trails are steep. The staircase into Hurricane Falls has 590 steps. The rock found in the gorge has been polished for ages by the Tallulah River. It is very slick to begin with, and more so when wet.

Rules for Gorge Floor Access *(Borrowed from park literature.)*

• Gorge Floor access is not permitted upstream beyond Hurricane Falls.

• Alcohol and other intoxicants, drink cans, glass bottles, firearms, fireworks and campfires are prohibited.

• Do not climb around any waterfalls, except Bridal Veil (Sliding Rock) at the base of the Sliding Rock Trail. Swimming is permitted at Sliding Rock *only*.

• Do not hike into the gorge if you are in poor health or are unaccustomed to strenuous exercise. *Those with weak hearts or weak knees should avoid the gorge.*

• Carry plenty of drinking water because gorge water is unsafe to drink.

• Beware of flash flooding. If Tallulah Falls Lake fills beyond storage capacity, water is released over the dam causing flooding in the gorge. Under normal conditions a siren sounds before release, however, you will not hear this unless you are near the dam. If flash flooding occurs, immediately move to higher ground.

Hurricane Falls is the most beautiful fall in the park. It ranks in my top five for scenery in Georgia. On my first visit to Hurricane, I spent six hours trying to catch it in the right light. Part of that time was waiting out a "hurricane" of a thunderstorm. Believe me, a clap of thunder echoes and is enhanced many times over as it reverberates off the gorge walls.

I completely understand why there is no access allowed (no permits issued) into the gorge while it is raining. During the storm that I endured, the river did not rise appreciably, but the quartz bedrock and boulders became treacherously slick with the first drop of rain. I found it impossible to stand atop it.

During water releases, Tempesta puts up massive clouds of mist that wet everything around *it* and for several hundred feet downstream. The water's of Hurricane crash and splash in pulsing jets, hammering the north gorge wall with such force, that they are vaporized into wind-whipped clouds of mist. Bridal Veil slides over smooth bedrock with enough force to capture air bubbles and take them deeply under. When sufficient air has collected, to overcome being submerged, it bursts to the surface in a fizzing, boiling surge.

Gorge Loop: Routed in this manner, the Sliding Rock and Hurricane Falls trails form a difficult 1.1 mile loop into and out of the gorge. The following is a brief description:

The Sliding Rock Trail (formerly known as the Wallenda Walk Trail) is very steep, treading a ridge line, via boulders and bedrock. These boulders form uneven steps. The South Wallenda Tower marks the beginning point for its descent into the gorge. This is a tough trail, indeed, that gives the seldom-used upper calves quite a workout. In spite of its short length, this trail is a contender for the most difficult in Georgia. Occasional window-like openings present beautiful views of the gorge's north rim.

Crossing the river upstream from Bridal Veil, and later, downstream from Hurricane, presents a challenge, even during periods of low water. During my in-gorge hikes, the river level was exceptionally low and the exposed boulders were spaced just about right at both crossings. I did, however, take my boots and socks off at both crossings and make a shallow wade where the boulders were spaced a little too far apart for rock hopping.

Between the aforementioned falls, the trail is more like a rocky, woodland path—easy to locate in places and in others it seems to vanish. There is one vast open area. This is in *front of* and *beside* Oceana Falls. The smooth bedrock is extremely slick here.

Shortline Trail: This paved hiking/cycling trail runs atop the grade of the historic Tallulah Falls Railroad for more than half its length. In the railroad's cuts, ferns and shade tolerant plants abound. Crossing the Tallulah River via a suspension bridge (.95 of a mile), the trail terminates at Old U. S. 441.

Terrora Trail (Upper Loop): This is a moderately rated woodland hike that branches off the Shortline Trail. For those seeking a slower pace this is a good place to get away from the crowds.

Jail Trail (Lake Loop): This trail begins at the Shortline Trail parking area. It soon becomes a pleasant shoreline walk beside a quiet cove of Tallulah Falls Lake. Fall's colors reflect beautifully in these peaceful waters. The trail passes the historic Tallulah Falls Jail then adopts Old U. S. 441 to complete the loop.

Stoneplace Trail: A 5.0 mile hiking/mountain biking trail that accesses Tugaloo Lake. A 4-WD road (Stoneplace Road) provides shuttle access.

Other Books by the Author
WATERFALL WALKS and DRIVES
in the
GREAT SMOKY MOUNTAINS
and the
WESTERN CAROLINAS
ISBN 0-9636070-3-0

A complete guide to the waterfalls of the Great Smoky Mountains National Park, and North and South Carolina's National Forests. Fifty-five day hikes leading to more than 125 of the region's most scenic waterfalls. One hundred fifty six pages of detailed driving and hiking directions. More than 70 topographic hiking maps with text keyed to them. Eight pages of color photos and easy instructions on how to photograph waterfalls.

Available at book and outdoor stores in the Southeast, or send check or money order for $9.95 to:

H.F. Publishing, Inc.
4552 E. Elmhurst Dr.
Suite "A"
Douglasville, Ga. 30135

Please add $2.00 shipping and handling per address. Please allow 4 weeks for delivery. Georgia residents add 6% sales tax.